Making Disciples, Making Leaders

Making Disciples, Making Leaders

A Manual for Developing Church Officers

Steven P. Eason

Foreword by William H. Willimon
Lesson Plans by E. Von Clemans

GENEVA

Book design by Teri Vinson
Cover design by Lisa Buckley

First edition
Published by Geneva Press
Louisville, Kentucky

This book is printed on acid-free paper that meets the American National Standards Institute Z39.48 standard. ♾

PRINTED IN THE UNITED STATES OF AMERICA

04 05 06 07 08 09 10 11 12 13 — 10 9 8 7 6 5 4 3 2 1

Library of Congress Cataloging-in-Publication Data

Eason, Steven P.
    Making disciples, making leaders : a manual for developing church officers / Steven P. Eason ; foreword by William H. Willimon ; lesson plans by E. Von Clemans.—1st ed.
        p. cm.
    Includes bibliographical references.
    ISBN 0-664-50263-6 (alk. paper)
    1. Church officers—Training of.   2. Christian leadership—Presbyterian Church (U.S.A.)—Study and teaching.   I. Title.

BX8969.6.E27 2004
253'.088'285137—dc22   2004041158

In memory of my father,
The Reverend William Everette Eason, Sr.

Contents

Foreword

Leadership is all the rage on college campuses these days. We now have courses in leadership, leadership institutes, professors of leadership studies, and all the rest. I confess that I am a bit suspicious of this new leadership craze on campus. Sometimes I wonder if these leadership courses and leadership professors are not simply there to flatter the self-image of our students. Every student who comes to our university thinks of himself or herself as a leader. They are all preparing themselves for positions of leadership, never for positions of subordination. Garry Wills, in his good book on the great leaders of history, *Certain Trumpets: The Call of Leaders*, says that good leaders are mainly a matter of people who have willing and able followers. Around here, however, if I were to teach a course in "How to Spend a Lifetime as a Really Good Follower," registration would be low.

Perhaps this new interest in leadership is a result of the widespread awareness that we really do have a problem with leadership in our society at present. With malfeasance among business leaders, incompetence and prevarication among some of our government leaders, to say nothing about the leadership scandals in the church, it is probably high time to turn our attention toward those who lead us.

I recently surveyed members of my denomination, asking them what qualities they looked for in a bishop for the United Methodist Church. (Presbyterians do not believe in bishops, but I have actually seen them.) I was impressed that the number-one quality that people seem to see in a bishop is "an ability to lead." It does not seem to me too radical an idea that a leader ought to be able to lead, but perhaps the current state of leadership has made that important to emphasize. You have a society full of managers rather than leaders, directors of the status quo, oilers of organizational machinery, those who see leadership as that which commands rather than serves—well, no wonder we turn our attention to leadership. Where does leadership come from, how is it characterized, what qualities make for a good leader, and how do you do it?

Steve Eason has written a wonderful book on leadership in the church. Perhaps the most wonderful thing about Steve's book is that this book is clearly, unashamedly, pointedly about leadership *in the church*. He begins, not with a treatise on organization, or even by focusing upon the characteristics of leaders, but rather in worship. The church is a creation not of our savvy organizational ability, but of God. Good leadership in the church, Steve implies, is a gracious, creative act of God.

Too much thinking about leadership in the church takes its cue from essentially secular models of leadership, letting business or politics set the tone, failing to appreciate the uniquely theological basis of the church. When we think about leadership in the church, we must do more than simply put a sort of Christian veneer over essentially godless concepts borrowed from business or wherever. We must begin by noting the particular vocation, formation, and expectation of the church, which Steve does beautifully.

Furthermore, Steve takes care to make this book particularly, peculiarly Reformed. From what I have seen, good leadership is never leadership in general—abstract principles that are universally applied despite the specific context. Steve writes a most Presbyterian book. (By the way, Steve began as a Methodist, but then he took my class at Duke Divinity School, and shortly thereafter became a Presbyterian! He was probably too creative and energetic for us anyway.) In this book, Steve, despite having been a Presbyterian pastor for more than twenty years, retains a new convert's love of the Reformed faith. As one who was discovered by the Reformed tradition, rather than born into it, Steve has a unique and keen perspective of the virtues of that faith.

The Reformed tradition was, in part, a creative rediscovery of peculiarly biblically based, theologically formed leadership. While the church is of God—a gift in each generation from a God who does not leave us to our own devices—the church is also the people of God. This peculiar people rely upon more than hierarchy and tradition for their formation. The Reformed faith envisions the church as a congregation that depends upon the Holy Spirit raising up those, in every generation, who are called to leadership of the church. Steve's book embodies that Reformed vision beautifully.

Yet, Steve not only gives us a perspective—a theologically based vision of leadership—but also a very practical, pragmatic guide for energizing a church in mission and ministry. In other words, the real beauty of this book is that Steve not only tells us where to go, but also how to get there. In his fine book on leadership, *Leadership without Easy Answers*, Ronald Heifetz of Harvard stresses that leaders are always teachers. Leaders have the responsibility to keep feeding information into an organization, to keep training members of the organization to perform their legitimate leadership functions, and to keep refurbishing and refueling the organization's vision for itself. In this book Steve keeps calling modern Presbyterians to, in effect, recover their birthright of informed, intellectually formed spirituality. He also models this through a sort of recovery of the office of the teaching elder.

Used by individual pastors or elders, or studied in the session, this book offers an entire program of renewal that is theologically based and realistically workable. Many a congregation will find itself renewed through Steve's good guid-ance. Many a pastor will gain the skills that are needed to lead in a way that is faithful to the Reformed tradition and up to the challenge of the present age.

I may not be the greatest theological professor in the world, but I certainly did a good work when I got Steve to leave my church for leadership among the Presbyterians!

William H. Willimon
Dean of the Chapel and Professor
  of Christian Ministry
Duke University
Durham, North Carolina

Acknowledgments

I am very grateful to Joe Donahoe who served as pastor of the Eastminster Presbyterian Church in Columbia, South Carolina, for encouraging me to spend a lot of my time developing leadership.

The congregations of First Presbyterian Church, Morganton, North Carolina, Mount Pleasant Presbyterian Church, Mount Pleasant, South Carolina, and Myers Park Presbyterian Church, Charlotte, North Carolina, have all contributed to this work. Without them there would be no book.

Von Clemans's role as educator strengthened the lesson plans, teaching resources, and exam. It's just more fun to work on a team.

Thanks to Lynn Turnage for suggesting my work to Geneva Press. Thank God for Suzanne Barber, my administrative assistant, who knows how to spell and type. I am grateful to Will Willimon, who inspired me to design the worship component of this leadership development model.

Many thanks for my wife, Catherine, who has been an encourager, listener, coach, and friend in ministry since the summer of 1976.

This has been a team effort. Thanks be to God.

Introduction

There's an old saying: "If you always do what you've always done, you'll always get what you've always got!" Sometimes, though, we seem to change what we're doing without being clear about our target. We just know that what we're doing isn't working, so we change it. What is it that we really want to accomplish?

The second of Stephen Covey's habits of highly effective people is "Begin with the End in Mind." He writes, "It's incredibly easy to get caught up in an activity trap, in the busy-ness of life, to work harder and harder at climbing the ladder of success only to discover it's leaning against the wrong wall."[1] What is the "end" that we, as the church, have in mind? Have we been "leaning against the wrong wall"?

A hardware store is clear about its business. You don't go in there for a gourmet meal. I am clear about what I am doing at the dry cleaners or the gas station. The hospital, the bank, the grocery store, and the doctor's office are all very clear about their business. Why do we seem to be less clear about the business of the church? Are we to gather more members, more money, more staff, and more programs? Are we there to comfort people, to provide hope and care? Are we there only to provide certain rites of passage, such as baptism, weddings, and funerals? Are we there for social change? What is the end we have in mind?

The Presbyterian Church (U.S.A.) has a trend of losing members. So, is one end to increase membership? A common question pastors hear is, "How big is your church?" I have started answering, "In what regard? Do you mean membership? We are thirty-eight hundred members. Do you mean attendance? We are averaging twelve hundred. Do you mean budget? We are just over 4 million. Facilities? 139,000 square feet. Do you mean in terms of discipleship? I am not quite sure how to measure that." Certainly discipleship was the end that Jesus had in mind.

The bigger questions that reflect the concern with discipleship are leadership questions:

- How big are we with regard to our faithfulness to Christ?

- How large is our church in terms of its love for God and neighbor?

1

- How big is our heart?
- How committed are we to the lordship of Christ, to equipping the saints for the work of ministry?

What questions are your leaders asking? What end does your church have in mind?

Maybe if we could change the questions that leadership is asking, we could find some new direction. Maybe we could shift the end in mind from institutional maintenance to discipleship, to equipping saints for the work of ministry. This shift will not happen overnight, and it must begin with leadership.

Building a Team Concept and Selecting Strong Leaders

In his book *Pastor*, Will Willimon writes, "Too many pastors never rise above simple congregational maintenance. . . ."[2] It's very easy to stay busy with maintenance. We can fill up our time in meetings that are about as exciting as a cup of cold coffee. Maintenance meetings are boring. There has to be something more.

In 1993, I completed a doctor of ministry degree at Columbia Seminary in Decatur, Georgia. My dissertation was entitled *A Team Ministry Leadership Development Course*. The project stemmed from my observations from growing up in the manse (a United Methodist parsonage), pastoral counseling sessions with clergy and their families, and all the evidence that many clergy were burning out. I started out to do research on clergy burnout. I quickly discovered that most clergy don't want to talk about their fatigue or sense of failure, especially with other clergy. My next step was to back up. Instead of waiting for clergy to fall, what could we do to prevent burnout? What could we change that would make ministry more bearable, even exciting?

Everything I read was pointing to team ministry: empowering the laity, sharing leadership, equipping the saints. That approach made sense. A church can only be as strong as its leadership, and clergy cannot bear that burden alone. Chapter 1 in this book provides biblical evidence that the best leadership is team leadership.

I did the research and designed a new curriculum to train deacons and elders to be on a team with the pastor(s). I field-tested the course and had it evaluated by the student participants and some certified Christian educators. Then, for the next ten years, I taught the course, which has changed, evolved, gotten worse, then better. This book shows where I am now. It'll look different as soon as next year! I have shared everything I have learned over the past ten years from making mistakes in training deacons and elders. My students have been the best teachers.

Building a leadership team begins by choosing the best candidates. Chapter 2 on nominations committee work is brief but important. More work needs to be done with the nominations committee in order for us to have quality candidates for deacons and elders. Building a strong team begins with selection.

As Presbyterians, we have the perfect system for building a leadership team. We ordain elders and deacons to office. They are not just volunteers. They are called. They kneel before God and the congregation, take vows, and receive the laying on of hands. We are set up from the beginning to take this seriously. We can capitalize on our system of government. We are charged by the *Book of Order* to train our officers:

> The minutes of session shall record the completion of a period of study and preparation, after which the session shall examine them [deacons/elders] as to their personal faith; knowledge of the doctrine, government, and discipline contained in the Constitution of the church; and the duties of the office.[3]

Officer training is a teachable moment. Newly elected officers are usually motivated to learn. Most of them want their time as an officer to be a time of growth in their own faith. They want a deeper fellowship with other leaders in the church. They are open to learn more about the polity and theology of the church. Now is the time to set the bar high. You get what you ask for, and we have been asking for too little.

A New Leadership Training Model

If a church is only as strong as its leadership, then we need to spend more time and effort in strengthening the leadership of our church. Leadership development begins with the training.

What follows in chapters 3–7 of this book is a different model for training officers, encompassing worship, the Lord's Supper, Bible study, prayer, small groups, fellowship, theology, polity, and personal faith. It's all about team building. It's an empowerment model that takes seriously the parity of the call of elders, deacons, and ministers of the Word and Sacrament. The church will benefit from strengthening the leadership, and so will the world.

Formation vs. Information

When time constraints of ongoing church business are pressing and choices have to be made about how much and what to cover in officer development, the temptation is to avoid doing the difficult work of developing personal faith and to focus on covering the more objective framework and facts of the constitution.

If there is a deficiency in the lay leadership of today's church, if many who would serve as elders and deacons lack spiritual maturity, however, can those deficiencies be addressed by finding better ways to put more facts and information into the minds of church officers? Will being able to quote chapter and verse from the *Book of Order* or the *Book of Confessions* make individuals better leaders in the church or make them better disciples? Can the recital of the details of Presbyterian polity or the doctrines of Reformed theology ever compensate for an underdeveloped personal faith? No.

This model of officer development understands the development of the officer's personal faith as *the* business of the church and the absolutely essential prerequisite for faithful and effective leadership in the church. Accordingly, a great deal of the officer development process in this model is designed to nurture and develop each officer's personal faith. Sharing a meal together at each session joins us in the sacred tradition of food feeding faith (see chap. 3). Corporate worship sets the beginning of every time we gather together, grounding us in shared faith through Scripture (chap. 4), and the instructions for the leader assume that faith development is central to the learning process (chap. 5). In chapter 6 you will find four lesson plans for theology and polity. Each plan provides several options for the instructor. The sharing of personal faith experiences in small groups (chap. 7) binds us into a community of faith that recognizes individual variety within one common witness.

Spiritual formation, not instilling information, is at the center of this model. If *some* is good, then isn't *more* better? Why not eliminate all the content and focus solely on spiritual formation, on just developing personal faith?

One reason is found in our constitution. Personal faith is but one of five areas in which officers are to be examined. Our constitution requires that officers demonstrate a satisfactory working knowledge of the doctrine, government, and discipline of the church, as well as the duties of the office of elder and deacon. The lesson plans provided in chapter 6, which were developed by E. Von Clemans, cover all of these areas.

Another reason not to limit ourselves just to spiritual formation is located in the issue of our identity as Presbyterians. If we focused entirely on personal faith development, we might end up with highly developed spiritual persons, but they wouldn't necessarily be Presbyterian leaders.

Presbyterian Identity

Every three years, our denomination selects a group of Presbyterians to serve as The Presbyterian Panel. Each group is a representative sample of five thousand Presbyterians (members, elders, pastors, and specialized clergy) who serve for a three-year period. During this time, panel members are invited to respond to mailed questionnaires four times a year. The responses of the panel provide a glimpse into the backgrounds, practices, beliefs, and opinions of both clergy and laity in our church.

This research has shown recently that many of the members of our congregations, from which we choose church officers, have not been raised as Presbyterians. In the 2000–2002 panel, only 42 percent of Presbyterian members and elders grew up as Presbyterians.[4] For the 2003–2005 panel, the percentage was only slightly higher at 45 percent.[5] Unless your congregation chooses only born-and-bred Presbyterians as officers, more than half of your officers are likely to have been something other than Presbyterian in their childhood. In other words, many of our elders and deacons will not come into office with a built-in understanding of the Presbyterian Church, what it stands for, and how it works.

If the Presbyterian Church has anything valuable or distinctive to offer to Christians in the twenty-first century, its leaders will need to have a working knowledge of the specific beliefs and behaviors that make us who we are as Presbyterians.

Finding Balance

We must attend to both formation and information. In this model we focus on the spiritual formation of persons with a personal relationship to Jesus Christ as Lord, and we focus on providing officers with the information needed to serve as Presbyterian elders and deacons. We lean heavily on experiences and activities that foster personal spiritual growth. We also make sure, at the end, that each officer can articulate his or her knowledge of the doctrine, government, and discipline of the church, as well as the duties of his or her particular office.

In chapter 6, I select the four theology units from the first four ordination questions: the Lordship of Christ, authority of Scripture, essential tenets of the Reformed faith, and the Confessions. The polity units seek to cover the basics of the *Book of Order.* These sessions do not spend much time with the discipline section, but I strongly suggest that the class review it and know how to reference it.

Another significant contribution is the study guide to the *Book of Order*, which serves as the study sheet for the exam. The examination (chap. 8) procedure was something I inherited at Myers Park. Frankly, I had been letting folks off the hook by just having them share their faith stories. As powerful as that is, having to know the material is one more way to raise the bar.

The final chapters look to life with your new elders and deacons after the training sessions have been completed. Chapter 9 offers a new model for monthly session and diaconate meetings that helps to continue leadership development. Chapter 10 explores a host of ways to strengthen leadership among the staff, inactive elders, and committee chairs, as well as advocating continuing education for officers. Throughout the book, consideration is given to small churches.

In the conclusion to the book, my former students have their own say. I have included excerpts from deacons and elders from three of the churches I have served in order to convey some of the impact this new way of training officers has had in their lives. Their testimonies speak to the effectiveness of following this plan. You may want to read this section first to inspire you to make the commitment to this process.

One of the dangers of the institutional church is the temptation to spend all our energy in self-maintenance and survival. The church that has more members as its end in mind needs more members to get more pledge cards to have more money to build more buildings to hire more staff to do more programs to add more members to get more pledge cards. But for what? If you always do what you've always done, you'll always get what you've always got. We can all benefit from developing a stronger leadership team within our churches.

Chapter 1

A Biblical Model
for Team Leadership

According to Genesis 2:18, the only thing in all of creation that was "not good" was that man (humanity) was alone—disconnected, isolated, having no one with whom to share, detached. Even God apparently does not enjoy working alone, so much so that God stoops to work with folk like us. Think of the great leaders of the Bible, such as Abram, Sarai, Moses, David, Deborah, Jonah, Mary Magdalene, and Simon Peter. None of these are exactly star players. Even so, God chose to work with them, which is no small detail.

Leadership in the Old Testament

Old Testament leaders were not people who were merely volunteering to run yet another organization. They worked for and with God. Reread their stories, listening for their weaknesses and for their dependence upon God. *Each one of these leaders had to be empowered in order to be coworkers with God.* After all, none of us is born qualified to work with the God of all creation, the One who made heaven and earth. Nonetheless, God chooses to call forth, equip, support, and utilize human leadership as a means of accomplishing divine business. God builds a team.

Perhaps the most prominent example of team ministry within the Old Testament is that found in the account of Jethro's advice to Moses:

> "Why do you sit alone, while all the people stand around you from morning until evening? . . . You will surely wear yourself out. . . . For the task is too heavy for you; you cannot do it alone. . . . You should also look for able [people] . . . who fear God, are trustworthy, and hate dishonest gain; set such [people] over them as officers over thousands, hundreds, fifties and tens. . . . So it will be easier for you, and they will bear the burden with you. If you do this, and God so commands you, then you will be able to endure. . . ." (Exod. 18:14, 18, 21, 22–23)

It is not good to "sit alone" (v. 14). How many clergy, elders, or deacons do you think are "sitting alone," or feel that they are? If the goal, as Jethro states it, is "to endure" (v. 23), then leadership has to be shared. That's the "Jethro principle."

The Jethro principle does not really belong to Jethro, though. His comment to Moses was, "If you do this, and God so commands . . ." (v. 23). The implication is that God has observed Moses operating in solo fashion and has assessed that this leadership style cannot provide what is necessary. Thus God instituted shared leadership and team ministry as a provision of grace. The alternative was for Moses to continue operating in solo fashion and "wear [him]self out" (v. 18a). The apparent motive behind Jethro's (and God's) advice was to ward off failure, to secure success.

A record of Moses's prayer reveals his own frustration and hopelessness in operating alone:

> Moses heard the people weeping throughout their families, all at the entrances of their tents. Then the LORD became very angry, and Moses was displeased. So Moses said to the LORD, "Why have you treated your servant so badly? Why have I not found favor in your sight, that you lay the burden of all this people on me? Did I conceive all this people? Did I give birth to them, that you should say to me, 'Carry them in your bosom, as a nurse carries a sucking child,' to the land that you promised on oath to their ancestors? . . . I am not able to carry all this people alone, for they are too heavy for me. If this is the way you are going to treat me, put me to death at once—if I have found favor in your sight—and do not let me see my misery." (Num. 11:10–12, 14–15)

Moses prayed and God responded. Moses was directed to recruit seventy of the elders of Israel and bring them to the tent of meeting, where God would do the rest:

> I will take some of the spirit that is on you and put it on them; and they shall bear the burden of the people along with you so that you will not bear it all by yourself. (Num. 11:17)

God empowers leadership, but we have to get ourselves to the tent of meeting. We have to position ourselves for empowerment. Empowerment is not a program or even a training course. It's a gift from God. Though we cannot achieve it, we do need to receive it. Our posture for receptivity is critical.

The team was empowered together. God didn't select the seventy and empower them in the privacy of their own homes. Moses selected the seventy and God empowered them with the spirit at the tent of meeting—together, in one place. Leadership is communal. By God's design, human leadership is recruited and equipped to participate with God in the task of leading and guiding the people. God's covenant with Abraham was a sharing of leadership. Israel's history of judges, kings, and prophets reflects God's choice to work with others toward the common goal of retrieving a lost humanity. In the Old Testament God clearly chooses not to act alone, and God does not intend for human leadership to act alone.

Leadership in the New Testament

If I had been Jesus, I would have definitely chosen to work alone! The disciples were always in the way. If you can multiply five loaves and two fish to feed over five thousand people, why do you need a bunch of riff-raff getting in your way?

Herein lies the principle. God chooses to work on a team, even if—and, perhaps especially, when—the team is dysfunctional. There's hope for any session!

Christ called twelve students. He intentionally recruited each one of them. All of them were busy. None of them had previous skills in being a leader in the church. They weren't volunteers; they were disciples—students, people going to school to obtain skill and knowledge. They weren't clergy. Jesus took fishermen, tax collectors, political activists, and businessmen to build his team. He took people with the potential for learning. He saw that potential in them and called it forth, even when they didn't see it themselves. Jesus charged the twelve with the task of leading the church, but always in the context of partnership with him:

> "Go therefore and make disciples of all nations, baptizing them . . . and teaching them to obey everything that I have commanded you. And remember, I am with you always. . . ." (Matt. 28:19–20)

Jesus shared leadership. He intentionally created a team for ministry. He did not work alone, and neither did they. Although he never spoke to this issue, a reader can deduce that his intentions were to equip a small group so that it could service a larger group. Moreover, leadership development was a key to Jesus's strategy for mission and ministry.

A prime example of the team ministry philosophy of Christ is found within the story of the feeding of the five thousand (Mark 6:30–44). Jesus has taken the disciples away to rest, but when they get out of the boat, they are met with more demands and needs. The disciples immediately draw up a plan to dismiss the crowds because of the late hour and the probability that food could be found in nearby villages.

Note Jesus's response to their plan: "You give them something to eat" (Mark 6:37a). Everyone sees the obvious impossibility of this task; nevertheless, Jesus puts the privilege of ministry on the twelve. They respond with apparent sarcasm: "Are we to spend a year's salary on this group?" (v. 37). Jesus replies: "How many loaves have you? Go and see" (v. 38). Jesus looked to them to provide the base resources from which a miracle would grow.

Once they had surrendered their meager resources—five loaves and two fish—to Christ, by the power of God provisions were made for the five-thousand-plus people who were present. Christ took the resources, looked beyond the human realm to heaven, and then "blessed and broke the loaves" (v. 41a), but the twelve had gathered the resources in the first place.

Notice the next move of Christ: "he gave [the multiplied fish and loaves] to his disciples to set before the people" (6:41b). Jesus used the disciples in team fashion to serve the people. Again, he pulls his followers into the experience. Jesus's floating the food out to the folk would have been quicker and more impressive. Using human resources took a lot longer, but the disciples/students would have missed sharing the experience. When all had eaten, they took up twelve baskets of leftovers. That's one basket per disciple. Their own personal needs were provided for in abundance, just as they provided for others. Notice, though, that Jesus makes number thirteen on the team. The others had to feed him out of their own baskets. Imagine that!

Some may read this story and marvel at the ability of Jesus to multiply fish. An underlying and perhaps more significant lesson is revealed if you watch the inter-relatedness of Christ with the world (the five thousand), with his disciples, and the disciples with the world. This obvious team effort is clearly by Christ's design and by God's empowerment. The story begs us to ask of ourselves, *What are our resources? What do we have to offer that Christ can use?*

Implications for the Presbyterian Church (U.S.A.)

You very rarely hear anyone complaining about our system of government. They may not like some of the actions taken, but you will probably never hear anyone say, "Let's get rid of the elders, the session, the deacons." We like our system. It's biblical, and in spite of us, it works.

We struggle with some things. We appear awkward when it comes to the empowerment part of leadership. We can recruit and we even take a stab at training, but what about empowerment? Where does that happen for deacons and elders and clergy? Empowerment is so key in the biblical accounts and yet so missing in our story. The typical training class of new officers is centered on the *Book of Order*. Teach them the rules only, though, and what you have is a bunch of rule-keepers. That's not leadership. It's sure not empowered leadership. It's management, at best.

Have we committed the sin of taking lawyers, bankers, doctors, homemakers, teachers, and businesspeople and asking them to run the church without empowerment? For three years, these volunteers slave at their leadership task, and when done, many of them vow to never return. Why? No empowerment. The work is too task-oriented. We fail to see the leadership team as a community of faith that needs to be nurtured and cultivated.

Those of us who are clergy need to take our lay leaders, our team, with us to the tent of meeting. We need the Spirit dispensed upon us together. They need to share what we have (or what we are supposed to have), and we need what they have to offer. Regarding leadership in the church, the Bible teaches that God calls us to work and serve together.

Chapter 2

Choosing the Team: Nominations

Moses had to select seventy officers. Jesus hand-picked twelve disciples. How much time do we spend with the nominations committee?

In most cases, members of the nominations committee don't spend much time with each other. In a typical year, they usually do not meet until September or October unless a resignation occurs or a new position is to be filled. The standing task of their autumn meeting is to form a slate of officers. They go through their procedure, make calls, nail the slate down, and never meet as a group again.

This limited schedule and activity can imply that the work of the nominations committee is routine and not necessarily important. The truth is just the opposite! The work of this committee is the first place to begin changing the way your church does business.

Developing healthy membership and procedures for the nominations committee is different from trying to control the nomination process. My suspicion is that a lot of clergy stay out of the process so as to not be accused of trying to control it. The coaching metaphor is one that I have found most helpful. Can you imagine the head basketball coach of a major university not being involved in the recruiting process? (I know pastors don't have the same kind of power as a head coach, but stay with me!) According to Ephesians 4:1–16, which is a text used in one of your training worship sessions, pastors are like coaches. Our task is to "equip the saints for the work of ministry" (v. 12). We don't do the work for them, nor do we stay detached. We "equip." We help identify gifts, and we recruit, train, and supervise leaders. In so doing, we equip the church for its work of ministry, which is building up the body of Christ.

Selecting a leadership team is similar to selecting any other kind of team. In basketball, not everyone needs to play center, and you don't need five point guards. The coach looks for diversity and balance. In addition, some players are more mature than others. Some players have paid more dues, worked harder, made more of a commitment. A good coach knows how to cultivate the best players and bring along the lesser ones. You coach them all.

The nominations committee is the key link to building an effective team. Not everyone is a strong player. Some folk have the potential, though, which is what you look for when you put together the slate of nominees. Because subsequent training and ongoing leadership development strengthens all the players, the nominations committee does not have to choose perfect people, just faithful ones.

Consider having the nominations committee meet monthly or every other month throughout the year. What would the members do at those meetings? They could pray more, review the procedures and dream about better ways to do the process, begin a list of potential officers, have present officers come to the meeting and talk about their experience in serving, or have the entire committee attend a deacons' meeting and a session meeting. They could space the deadlines so the work is not rushed. The church would certainly see a tremendous difference in the process of choosing officers.

Here is a suggested annual agenda that uses a January-to-December timetable. (The schedule should be adjusted, of course, depending on when your church elects its nominations committee. Whenever that may be, begin the next month with the organizational meeting that is listed below for January.)

January

• Take time to get to know each other. Have everyone share a description of the best deacon/elder they have ever known. Make notes. You are hoping to nominate those kinds of people.

• Have a half-hour Bible study using chapter 2 in this book. Read Exodus 18:17–18, 22–33; Numbers 11:10–12, 14–15; or Mark 6:30–44. Discuss some of the following three questions together:

> 1. Why do you think God would choose to use humans in shared leadership?

2. How would you compare what we look for in elders/deacons with what God asked Moses to look for in choosing leaders? (Num. 11:10–12, 14–15)

3. What lessons about discipleship do you learn from the story of the feeding of the five thousand?

• Consider having the group read a book together. A host of books are available on leadership in the church. I recommend Anthony B. Robinson's *Transforming Congregational Culture.*[1] Set aside some time at each meeting to discuss your readings.

• Feed the group.

• Always, at every meeting, pray for God's guidance together.

February

Have the entire nominations committee attend the February deacons' meeting. (Unicameral churches can skip this month.) Instruct them to make notes of attendance and to notice details such as the number of women, number of men, age differences, and so on. Ask them also to pay attention to the dynamics of the meeting. Who's in charge? How does the team work together? Who might need to be on this team to improve it? Finally, ask the committee to make note of who is rotating off this year. What kind of replacements are needed?

March

Attend the March session meeting with the same agenda as for the deacons' meeting.

April

Meet to compare notes on the meetings that the members attended in February and/or March. The group should start to see a vision for what and who are needed to serve. Make sure the clergy are present to hear these insights.

May

• Have an active elder and a deacon come to the meeting to share their perspectives of serving. It could be the clerk and the moderator of the deacons. Ask for the good, the bad, and the ugly. What kind of people do they think their teams need?

• Ask the deacons and elders as a whole to generate a list of nominees at their May meetings.

June

Meet before the summer break to go over the list of nominees that the elders and deacons provided in May. Make sure the nominating committee members add to this list with their own suggestions for nominees as well. Do this before you ask the congregation for names.

July

Plan this time as a month off, with no activities for the committee.

August

- In early August, solicit the congregation for nominee names.

- Ask each program staff person to put in names.

- Ask committee chairs for names.

- Ask the pastor(s) for names.

- Build the list and complete it by the end of the month. Meet to compile the names.

September

- Begin to build an A list, B list, and C list.

- Attempt to balance the diaconate and session with representatives of females, males, and age levels. Also pay attention to the various gifts that are needed.

- In this process, always consider the possibilities of those who would be newly ordained. Every class should include a percentage of new leadership. New blood helps the team and brings new life into the session and diaconate.

October

- Spend this month recruiting. Have members of the nominating committee see everyone on the A list. Do not recruit over the phone.

- Explain the expectations to each nominee, even former officers, because those expectations may have changed since they last served.

- Pray with the nominees, right there on the spot. After all, leadership is a calling that involves some discernment. Members of the committee will be better prepared to help the nominees with this discernment as a result of having attended the deacon and session meetings, studied Scripture, engaged in prayer, and interviewed staff and officers. They will know what they are talking about and can therefore more effectively call the nominees to serve.

November

Some folk may decline the call, so the committee will need time for calling others. A decline is not failure. It could be providential! Finish before Thanksgiving so that the committee can meet and give thanks!

December

- If the congregation's annual meeting is in January, use December as a month to have a party and present the slate as a courtesy to the deacons and elders.

- Publicize the slate to the congregation with biographical information on each candidate.

- Prepare for the election.

Several good resources for training nominations committees are available. In 1997, Eugene Witherspoon and Marvin Simmers edited a training manual titled *Called to Serve: A Workbook for Training Nominating Committees and Church Officers*.[2] They have a section dedicated to training a nominations committee that provides a very helpful structure, as well as resources. The work includes Bible study, prayer guidelines, agendas, case studies, and *Book of Order* references. The *Book of Order* drills are especially effective in getting your nominations committee exposed to the job before them.

One exercise in *Called to Serve*, "5 × 5," is of particular interest to me. The group performs five exercises, with five minutes allotted for each exercise. The five exercises are titled:

1. The Marks of a Good Member

2. The Kind of Person We Need to Be an Officer

3. The Responsibilities of the Officers

4. The Commitment the Officers Make

5. The Expectation Our Congregation Has of Our Officers.[3]

This exercise can be especially helpful for the nominating committee.

You may also want to obtain copies of a pamphlet by Edward K. Fretz titled *Nominating Church Officers.*[4] Although somewhat dated, Fretz's publication provides a good thumbnail sketch for the committee's work.

We would do well to spend more time with the nominating process. I know that God empowers leadership, but God told Moses to go select "seventy of the elders of Israel, whom you know to be the elders of the people and officers over them" (Num. 11:16). Our task is to bring qualified people for empowerment!

Chapter 3

An Overview
of the Training Course

The Officers' Training Committee

Most churches don't have an officers' training committee. I didn't have one until I came to Myers Park. I wouldn't do without one now! This particular committee is a subcommittee of our education council.

The officers' training committee is another example of team ministry taking the administrative burden off of the clergy's back. The committee's job is to

- See to ordering the necessary books and having them at the organizational meeting for distribution
- Prepare the communion for each training worship experience
- Take roll at each training meeting
- Contract the meals for all four sessions
- Collect money for the meal and see to clean-ups
- Produce and distribute handouts for each session

- Attend to examination, ordination, and installation details
- Make the small-group assignments and room designations
- Attend each training session as assistant to the pastor(s)

You can see how valuable the members of this committee are. Plus, having a committee designated for this task communicates to the new officers that congregation members take officer training seriously. The training sessions are also enhanced when the committee members act in service to the new officers.

The Organizational Meeting

Immediately after election, set a date and time for the organizational meeting. Tell everyone to bring their calendars. The purpose of this meeting is to schedule the four training sessions, each of which will last three-and-a-half hours. The goal for timing the meetings is achieving 100 percent attendance. In other words, don't settle for partial attendance at any training session. This goal is difficult but not impossible, and commitment to it builds from the outset. You may have to skip a week or two, and that's okay. When setting the dates, make sure the participants have enough time to do the reading and homework between training sessions. They have homework before the first session, so allow time for completing that as well.

Once you have negotiated the four training sessions (which is a team building exercise in and of itself), distribute the books and worksheets. Give the participants instructions on where to meet, go over the assignments, and pray! Make a note to send out a written reminder before the first session with instructions and a prompting to do the reading and assignments.

You will feel the energy after the organizational meeting. Peer pressure helps the participants make the sacrifices, do the work, show up at meetings, and take this whole thing a lot more seriously.

The Four Training Sessions

Each training session has five components: worship, theology, dinner, polity, and small groups. Here's the suggested schedule for each evening.

5:30–6:00 p.m.	Worship
6:00–6:45 p.m.	Theology
6:45–7:15 p.m.	Dinner
7:15–8:00 p.m.	Polity
8:00–8:45 p.m.	Small groups (personal faith)

Worksheet 1
Church Office Development Workshops: Overview and Assignments

UNIT	WORSHIP	THEOLOGY	MEAL	POLITY	SMALL GROUPS	ASSIGNMENTS
3 hours, 15 minutes	30 minutes	45 minutes	30 minutes	45 minutes	45 minutes	To be done *prior* to the class
#1	Moses gathers 70 elders Numbers 11:10–17	Jesus Christ is Lord		The PC(USA) Constitution Overview Presbyterian Principles	Models of Faith	☐ *Selected to Serve:* Chapters 1, 3 ☐ *Book of Order:* G-1 through G-4 ☐ **Study Guide:** 1.1–2.3, 3.1–3.3, 3.8 ☐ **Small Groups:** Models of Faith ☐ **Worksheet #2:** Jesus Christ is Lord ☐ **Worksheet #3:** Principles of Presbyterian Polity
#2	Jesus and the disciples feed the 5,000 Mark 6:30–44	The Understanding and Use of Holy Scripture		The Sacraments Directory for Worship	To Be a Christian	☐ *Selected to Serve:* Chapter 4, pp. 120–24 ☐ *Book of Order:* W-1, 2 ☐ *Book of Confessions:* 9.27–9.30 ☐ **Study Guide:** 4.1–4.8 ☐ **Small Groups:** To Be a Christian ☐ **Worksheet #4:** The Bible Tells Me So ☐ **Worksheet #5:** Worship/Sacrament Quiz
#3	The disciples receive the Holy Spirit Acts 1:8; 2:1–4, 43–47	Presbyterian/Reformed Tradition The Essential Tenets		Ordination Vows Duties of the Office	My Faith Inventory	☐ *Selected to Serve:* Chapters 5, 7, 8 ☐ *Book of Order:* G-6, G-10, G–14.0207 ☐ **Study Guide:** 2.11–2.15, 3.4–3.7 ☐ **Small Groups:** My Faith Inventory ☐ **Worksheet #6:** To Be or Not To Be Reformed ☐ **Worksheet #7:** Constitutional Questions
#4	The gifts of the Spirit Ephesians 4:11–16	The Confessions		How your church works; How to get things done	My Reflections and Goals for Faith Development	☐ *Selected to Serve:* Chapters 2, 6, 9 ☐ *Book of Order:* G-5, G-7, G-8; 9.0101–0104, 9.0200–0503, D-1 ☐ *Book of Confessions:* pp. xi–xxx; prefaces to each confession ☐ **Study Guide:** 2.4–2.10, 5.1–5.3, 6.1–6.8 ☐ **Small Groups:** My Reflections and Goals for Faith Development ☐ **Worksheet #8:** *Book of Confessions*

Each unit is allotted forty-five minutes except for worship and dinner. Adults need at least forty-five minutes to have an educational experience. Again, I encourage you not to shorten the program. Don't cut worship or dinner, which are both huge team builders.

Reference Materials

Reference materials are listed in the appendices. They are identified in the relevant chapters, and they include worship samples, theology and polity handouts, worksheets, and answer keys. For your quick reference, they are:

- Appendix A: Study Guide for New Elders and Deacons

- Appendix B: *Book of Confessions* Presentation Outline

- Appendix C: Worship Services for the Four Training Sessions

- Appendix D: Theology and Polity Worksheets and Handouts

- Appendix E: Small-Group Worksheets

- Appendix F: Miscellaneous Correspondence and Forms

- Appendix G: Resources for Church Officer Development

The Meal

Have dinner together. If you adapt the schedule to Saturday mornings, have lunch together. The meal does something for the groups. You might not need instructions for preparing a meal, but here are six things we have learned:

1. The setting is important. The fellowship hall is the logical place, but we have also had the meal in our main classroom, which saves time.

2. Use a caterer or have church volunteers bring in the meal. Have a good menu. No sandwiches! Treat the team to a good meal. They will feel the appreciation and respond with gratitude.

3. We like round tables. The tables should be set up so folks can talk to each other. Use centerpieces and tablecloths—make it special.

4. We play music during dinner to set the mood. Start putting something into the leaders, and you will be amazed what you get out!

5. They can pay for the meal, but it's even better to budget it under "officer training."

6. The bottom line is fellowship. Use name tags. I know sessions and diaconates where the people don't even know each other. Mealtime fellowship puts an end to that. Participants will love it, and you will enjoy it too. Everyone will leave with a good taste in their mouths!

On my schedule, dinner is set for 6:45 p.m. In that scenario, the participants have been here since 5:30 p.m. They have had a vibrant worship experience and discussed theology. Dinner gives them a chance to rest, assimilate what they have learned so far, and move around a bit. The meal serves to refresh their bodies, minds, and spirits. Afterward, officers in training will be ready for some polity and small groups!

You can set up another schedule, but try not to go too late. The energy level diminishes with later hours. Some folks may not be able to get off work to be there at 5:30 p.m. You be the judge, but I have found that people can meet this schedule when the need arises. This gathering is every bit as important as a doctor's appointment. Stay with it. We have found Sunday evenings to be the best.

Smaller Churches

What about small churches? An estimated 80 percent of the PC(USA) is composed of small churches (three hundred members or less). If that's true, a lot of our churches are either unicameral in structure or have a limited number of people serving on the diaconate and session. A training class for new elders and deacons would be even smaller. What if you only have three elders and three deacons in a class, or fewer? This format seems to be overkill in that situation. Building a sense of excitement with so few people would be difficult. (The minimal number of participants I'd consider would be six.)

Small churches might want to consider doing this training with one or more other small churches in your area. Presbyterians often use the cluster method for training officers in small churches. This course could easily be adapted to such a model. Clergy could share training responsibilities, and the group could rotate meetings around the churches. You could also do this course once for your entire session and diaconate, and then go to the cluster idea with other churches.

This material can easily be adapted to a weekend retreat or a daylong Saturday event, as described below. The downside of a retreat is the lack of reading and homework and the loss of the small-group experience. You will also miss the four worship services. All of our reviews over the years have given the highest marks to the worship experience and small groups. A retreat is better than nothing, but consider the pros and cons seriously before going that route.

Can We Do This in a Retreat?

If a retreat seems to be the best solution for your church (or churches), I recommend that you have a Friday evening/Saturday timetable. An off-site location would be best, but you could always have it at the church. The following outline is only a suggestion. You can plug in any of the resources for worship, theology, polity, and small groups. Provide the participants with the necessary worksheets and reading assignments prior to the retreat so they can be prepared.

Friday

6:00 p.m.	Gathering/refreshments
6:30	Dinner
7:15	Worship (Num. 11:10–17)
7:45	Theology 1: "Jesus Christ Is Lord" (see handouts)
8:30	Small groups (Handout: "My Models for Faith Development")
9:15	Free time

Saturday

8:30 a.m.	Breakfast
9:15	Worship (Mark 6:30–44)
9:45	Polity 1: Constitution Overview—Principles
10:30	Break
10:45	Theology 2: "The Essential Tenets of the Reformed Faith"
11:30	Lunch
12:15	Polity 2: Ordination Vows—Duties of the Office
1:00	Small groups: "My Reflections and Goals for Faith Development"
1:45	Closing

This format allows you to experience two parts of each of the original training sessions, drawing on the components of worship, theology, polity, meals, and small groups. Those sections that you did not have time to cover at the retreat could be used at other times as continuing education for the officers.

A One-Day Event

A one-day event could be easily organized by expanding the Saturday schedule to include another theology unit. Again, the downside of condensing the experience is the lack of preparation time to read the material, fill out the worksheets, and so on. You also miss building on the small-group experience, something that has proven valuable to participants in the past. Even so, something is better than nothing. You know your situation best.

Chapter 4

Begin with Worship

Training officers to worship has changed the way our deacons and elders see their role in the church. I begin each training session with a half-hour Communion service in the sanctuary. That's important. We begin at the table with the baptismal font in sight.

Go to the sanctuary. Go to the tent of meeting! If the elders and deacons can't break bread together, how can we expect the congregation to do it? If the leaders of the church can't pray together, how will the congregation come to it? The leadership team is a microcosm of the church. God empowered the seventy elders at the tent of meeting. Jesus empowered the twelve to empower the rest.

Worship and sacraments drape our identity as Christians. The leaders are fed here, and those of us who serve Communion to the people commune here. This is the fueling station, the Upper Room, the time with Jesus—and is much more than a little devotional we check off to get our real meeting started. This service *is* the real meeting. Most of the folks who have taken this course over the past ten years have identified the worship experience as one of the most meaningful aspects of the training. As a result, this practice of worshiping together as leaders has spilled over into our regular meetings. We begin every diaconate and session meeting in the sanctuary around the table.

If worship is done poorly, no one is empowered and God is probably bored. Too much structure can kill this moment; too little structure can create chaos. Every congregation has its own style of worship that needs to be integrated into this experience. Whatever you do, be creative, participatory, and stay within the time frame. If the worship service drags on, the participants will want to cut it out. The tent of meeting is a place where the Spirit shows up and empowers people for ministry. Hold onto that!

The Setting

Find a way to hold this service in your sanctuary. That room is where we make our commitments—where we take our wedding and baptismal vows, celebrate the Lord's Supper, worship together, and celebrate funerals. New officers are ordained here. It is a powerful space.

In our church, we use folding chairs to avoid having folks lined up in the pews. That way they can face each other in a circle or semicircle. The table is the focal point. To serve Communion, you might want to use intinction, which is easier and more personal. The empty pews remind us of the congregation, whom we have been chosen to serve. The pews are friendly reminders of our calling.

The Format

This simple outline works for us:

Call to worship

Hymn (Yes, we do sing!)

Prayer of confession/assurance of pardon

Scripture reading

Discussion of the text

Prayers/Lord's Prayer

Communion

Benediction

[See appendix C for Order of Worship samples.]

The *call to worship* is simply, "The Lord be with you." The people respond: "And also with you." They know this by heart, and it truly works as a call to worship.

A *hymn* is optional. If you have a small group, singing may be difficult. They often end up with more of a "joyful noise"! At our church, however, we sing even in the regular meetings of deacons and elders. The numbers are there, and it pulls us together.

The *prayer of confession* offers a wonderful opportunity to be creative. Sometimes I write the prayer on a handout to be read in unison or responsively. Sometimes I pass the baptism bowl with water in it. In silence we confess our sin as we are reminded of our baptism. I have passed a crown of thorns during Lent, the Christ candle during Advent, and anything else that might awaken our senses to confession.

We have only one *Scripture reading,* and I always print it on a handout. We use a variety of ways to read it: in unison, in parts, men/women, a preselected reader. Varying the form of presentation helps the participants hear the Word with fresh ears. If they appreciate these creative readings, an easy transition to do this can be made with the congregation on a Sunday morning. You will have a host of advocates out there applauding the change!

I always choose a text that I think speaks to leadership. Here are some samples:

Genesis 12:1–9	The call of Abram/Sarai
Genesis 22:1–18	The test of Abraham
Exodus 3:1–14	The call of Moses
Exodus 14:10–31	The Red Sea
Exodus 16	The manna
Exodus 18	Jethro's advice
Exodus 32	The golden calf
Exodus 33:7–23	The tent of meeting
Numbers 11:4–17	The seventy elders
Deuteronomy 8:10–20	Don't forget
Judges 6	Gideon—being reduced
1 Samuel 16	The call of David
2 Chronicles 7:11–16	"If my people . . ."
Job 38–42 (selected)	Knowing your place
Psalm 51	The sins of leadership
Ecclesiastes 3:1–8	Timing
Jeremiah 32:1–15	Jeremiah's field

Micah 6:8	What does the Lord require?
Malachi 3:6–12	The tithe
Matthew 4:1–11	The temptation of Jesus
Matthew 8:18–22	The cost of discipleship
Matthew 10:1–42	Sending of the Twelve
Matthew 13:24–30	Parable of the weeds
Matthew 19:13–15	Jesus and children
Matthew 19:16–30	Young rich ruler
Mark 4:1–20	The parable of the sower
Mark 6:30–44	Feeding of five thousand
Luke 5:17–26	Healing of a paralytic
Luke 10:38–42	Mary and Martha
Luke 21:1–4	The widow's example
Luke 24:1–12	The resurrection
John 3:1–21	Nicodemus
John 15:1–17	The vine and the branches
Acts 2	Pentecost
Acts 7:54–60	The stoning of Stephen
Acts 9:1–9	Saul's conversion
Ephesians 4:1–16	The offices of leadership
1 Timothy 3:1–13	Qualifications for the office
James 5:13–16	Prayer

You can also simply use the lectionary texts for the upcoming Sunday, especially if you plan to preach from them. The leadership team can help form the sermon! After the text has been read, I like to sit down as I ask the question, "What does this passage say to us as leaders of the church?" Then I wait. They will discuss the text. If I am not standing up in front, they have to talk with each other. Again, we are building a team. This tactic keeps the participants from looking to the leader for the answers.

Prayer comes next. After a brief discussion of the text, I remain seated and suggest we pray. I often invite them to say their prayers aloud, with the group responding after each speaker with "Lord, hear our prayer." Whatever you do, don't pray for them. Whatever method you use, let them do the praying. They can and will do it. Close with the Lord's Prayer.

Communion is simple. We don't use a formal liturgy in this setting. I, or one of the other pastors, say the words of institution, and the elders/deacons distribute the bread, saying, "The body of Christ broken for you." Then they pass the cup, saying, "The blood of Christ shed for you." We priest each other. Sometimes we sing "Let Us Break Bread Together," because we know it by heart. A benediction is offered, and off we go.

Worship serves as transition. It moves us from the world we have been in all day to another place with God. Worship says we are not here just to learn the *Book of Order* or run the church. It says we are not volunteers. The office we hold is not a gift because we have been here a long time, are popular, have a lot of money, or whatever other lame reason we can claim. Worship transforms us, empowers us, reclaims us, unites us, humbles us, cleanses us, but more importantly, it gives something to God—us.

Chapter 5

Teaching Tips

Adult Learners

If left to our instincts, most of us are likely to teach as we ourselves were taught as children. Often, however, this approach is not the best for teaching adults. Certain conditions for learning provide the optimal experience for adult learners. The following is a list of these conditions adapted from *The Kerygma Program Guide*,[1] along with some implications for teaching and learning as applied in this model of officer training.

Adults learn best and are most involved when they . . .

1. Are responsible for their own learning (that is, when they are not dependent on the leader as the only expert, authority, and primary source of information). In this model, we assume each officer is intelligent and capable of—individually and with others—finding factual answers in and discerning meaning from the resource material. Leaders resist being an expert answer giver and instead empower learners with the tools and confidence to find answers on their own.

2. Can participate directly in the process of their own learning (that is, by making decisions about what and how they will learn, and interacting with the subject matter and other learners). In this model, leaders provide options for learners, as well as multiple approaches and activities.

3. Are treated as individuals in a setting where differences are valued and respected (that is, when they are exposed to a variety of teaching/learning styles and are encouraged to work at their own pace and to make applications that are appropriate to themselves). In this model, respect for each learner—at all levels of experience, knowledge, or maturity—is paramount. Leaders provide a learning environment where the expression of and acceptance of differences is expected and encouraged.

4. Have opportunity to practice skills and express ideas and learnings in their own words (that is, when they can express personal insights and interpretation in words and in tangible application). In this model, learners will have regular opportunities to wrestle with and articulate their opinions and understandings individually before sharing them with others in a group.

5. Are within an environment of trusting relationships (that is, when learners are helped to become caring and supportive of other learners, and are encouraged to share feelings, needs, and concerns, as well as information and ideas). In this model, leaders demonstrate by example the kind of relationships they desire among the learners and create an atmosphere of openness to each individual's perspective. Leaders gently guide the group in maintaining a supportive environment.

6. Are not in competition with other learners (that is, when motivation comes through activities and resources that facilitate a cooperative, collaborative style of learning). In this model, learners work in groups to discuss individual insights and questions. Activities are designed to create win-win rather than win-lose outcomes.

7. Are exposed to strategies that enhance their own (and others') self-worth. In this model, learning activities are designed not to embarrass or highlight lack of knowledge or experience. Leaders encourage each learner and find something of value in each learner's comment, response, or question.

8. Gain a sense of satisfaction and experience success in the process of their learning. In this model, teaching strategies and activities are designed so that learners can and do achieve satisfaction and success instead of experiencing frustration.

Each of these conditions contributes to an optimal learning environment.

Limitations

One of the primary limitations of this model is time. The longest teaching segment of these workshops is only forty-five minutes long. Thus, in addition to worship, meal time, and small-group time, only eight forty-five-minute segments—six hours total—are available to cover everything needed in polity and theology.

To cover these content areas adequately would require far more than three hours each. So some decisions have to be made as to how to make use of this time.

The Learning Space

The kind of space your group needs depends, of course, on how many officers are participating in the program.

Here are some issues to consider:

- Use a space that will be relatively undisturbed throughout each evening.

- Ideally, everything except the faith-sharing groups will take place in the same space.

- Use a space large enough to accommodate discussions with the whole class, as well as those times when learners will be working with four or five others around a table.

- If possible, set up for dinner and eat your meal in your meeting space. In this fashion, the transition time to and from dinner (only thirty minutes) is as short as possible.

- If possible, use an open square so everyone can see each other. A chevron pattern is also workable. Avoid straight rows of tables where many are facing others' backs.

- Have extra pencils or pens handy, along with some writing paper, for those who might need them.

- Anytime a group of adults meets for this length of time, providing beverages and, if desired, a selection of snacks in the meeting room is a good idea. Learners can then help themselves as needed.

Leader Preparation

Leaders need to prepare for the workshops along with the learners. This book assumes that leaders of this model are either pastors or educators with a background in the polity and theology of the Presbyterian/Reformed tradition. These leaders provide the framework for the model; they also supply the participants with lesson plans, worksheets, handouts, and a bibliography of resources that has been custom-designed (or, at least, custom-selected from those provided in this book) to develop specific content as determined by their own wisdom and teaching style.

Additionally, because many important areas of theology and polity are not covered in this workshop model, you may want to think about a two-, or even three-year cycle of theology and polity topics. Leaders can use the overall model for the officer development program and adapt additional topics to meet the needs of a particular setting.

Handling Questions

If your experience is like that in my church, learners will have lots of questions throughout the course—some clarifying the assigned materials, many others on topics triggered by the discussions and assignments. The leader is often sorely tempted to respond to each of the questions as they arise. To do so, however, would likely take the whole class down paths not everyone would find helpful.

The leader's responsibility is to balance the need for an immediate response to questions over against the goal of working through the content as designed. Sometimes you need to defer a question until a later time, and sometimes you need to throw out the curriculum and capitalize on a more important interest. Only you can know the appropriate response.

Here are some suggestions, however, on how to handle the inevitable questions:

Collecting the Questions

- Give each learner a supply of three-by-five-inch index cards. Invite learners to write down questions as they occur and turn in the card at each class session.

- Post flip chart paper on the wall on which learners can write questions.

- Have a supply of Post-It notes handy. Let learners write their questions and post them on the black/whiteboard or on a flip chart.

- Provide a response sheet at each workshop for learners to use and turn in. In this way, you make sure learners are doing the assignments, and they have a vehicle for asking questions.

Answering the Questions

- Carve five minutes out of each class session to respond to selected questions from the class. Be disciplined!

- Write your responses to selected questions in a FAQ (frequently asked questions) format. Either distribute this document each week or compile it for the end of the workshops.

- Save the questions and pose one or two of them at each meeting of your session or diaconate. Invite the more experienced officers to respond. (Be gentle if they don't know the answers. Think of these moments as opportunities for continuing education!)

Learner Preparation

Officers-elect could participate in this program without preparing for each class, but everyone would suffer. For maximum learning to take place, each participant should spend a significant amount of time in preparation for each class. Prior to each class there are assigned readings in *Called to Serve*, the *Book of Order*, and the *Book of Confessions,* as well as worksheets to complete and questions to answer in the study guide.

While each learner works at his or her own pace, at least two to three hours of preparation will likely be required for each class. This time commitment is quite significant, so make sure the newly elected officers know what is required.

Assignments in Advance

Again, in order to make the best use of the limited class time, each learner needs to receive all the assignments for the four sessions ahead of time, preferably at the organizational meeting. By copying the resources provided, you can prepare a packet of materials to be given to each participant at least one week prior to the first session. That packet should include:

- The overview chart with dates for workshops and assignments to be done before each class

- Worksheets to be completed according to the assignments

- Any other materials needed for your particular setting

While this model covers a lot of ground in a short period of time, my experience has been that—with the fast pace, varied activities, and an emphasis on personal spiritual growth as well as learning content—the process invigorates most learners and, instead of becoming bored, they wish there were more time together.

Required Resources for Learners

In addition to the "assignments packet" that you prepare for each participant, each learner needs the following:

- A Bible—You may want to talk about the merits of various translations and paraphrases of Scripture, but all Scripture passages quoted in the provided handouts are from the NRSV.

- A *Book of Order* and a *Book of Confession*—These are available at around $7.50 each from the Presbyterian Marketplace (Phone: 1-800-524-2612; Internet: http://www.pcusa.org/marketplace/index.jsp). Online versions are available from the denomination's website for free download for those who can print their own. Check with your presbytery office each summer for any discounts that might be available as a result of bulk purchases through the presbytery.

- A copy of *Called to Serve*: *A Guide for Church Officers* by Earl S. Johnson Jr.—This publication is available for $14.95 from the Presbyterian Marketplace. Orders placed directly with the Presbyterian Publishing Corporation and using a church or pastor's account qualify for a discounted price. Orders can be made by phone at 1-800-227-2872 or online at www.ppcpub.com.

Chapter 6

Lesson Plans for Four Sessions on Theology and Polity

Lesson Plan for Session 1

The first lesson your officers experience begins with the primary affirmation of faith: Jesus Christ is Lord. Learners read and reflect on a biblical passage and see how the affirmation of the Lordship of Christ is at the center of the officer experience. They use their creative imaginations to put themselves in a situation where that affirmation is challenged by other "lords" and explore how the Christian Church has dealt with such challenges in the past. They review the constitutional claims that Jesus Christ is the Head of the Church and that God alone is Lord of the conscience, both in the sense of private discernment and in the experience of corporate judgment. Finally, the learners are introduced to a modern statement of the Lordship of Christ arising out of conflicts within the life of our denomination. You only have forty-five minutes, so you have to keep moving.

All handouts for the four sessions can be found in appendix D.

Learner Preparation

In order to make the most of the limited time, learners need to prepare for this lesson before you meet for the first time. Reading assignments are listed on the "Church Officer Development Workshops: Overview and Assignments" chart in chapter 3.

Learners need to have in advance the worksheet "Jesus Christ is Lord" (see appendix D) and, optionally, a copy of the paper *Hope in the Lord Jesus Christ*. The 214th General Assembly of the PC(USA) adopted this paper in response to multiple overtures to better understand the theological richness of the Lordship of Christ and it was commended to churches for study and reflection. Copies of the paper may be ordered from the Presbyterian Marketplace[1] or you may download a printable version of the paper, with study guide, from the denominational website.[2] Exposing the officers-elect to this paper is worthwhile but not necessary.

Leader Preparation

You need to familiarize yourself with the materials the learners are using to prepare for the lesson. As you work through the materials, try to anticipate questions or issues that the learners might have. For background material on the Romans Scripture passage in this context, the first chapter of the book *Witness without Parallel—Eight Biblical Texts That Make Us Presbyterian*, by Earl S. Johnson, is quite helpful.[3]

PART A: THEOLOGY—JESUS CHRIST IS LORD

Step 1 (ten minutes). Welcome everyone and take care of any housekeeping details as quickly as possible.

If you have enough people, divide your learners into groups of four or five persons. You need to keep the size of these discussion groups small. The more people in a group, the longer it takes for everyone to have a say. On the other hand, if your total group is four or less, dividing into smaller groups is unnecessary.

Step 2 (five minutes). Have each group discuss the questions from the lesson plan. Note that the learners should not be discussing their specific answers to the worksheet questions, but rather responding to the difficulty they most likely had in answering them.

Step 3 (three minutes). Give a mini-lecture on the significance of the Romans 10:9 passage from the standpoint of Presbyterian/Reformed theology. Use the suggestions in the lesson plan or develop your own points for presentation.

Step 4 (two minutes). Invite the learners to exercise their creative imaginations. In the form of a guided meditation, lead them through imagining they are a part of a small group of German Christians living during World War II in Nazi

Germany. Use word pictures and images to create a vivid scene of being a Christian under Nazi rule: What would it be like to see friends and neighbors captured and taken away? What would it be like to have the government proscribe your religious practice and compel the church to acknowledge a civil leader as ultimate authority? Once you have set this imaginary scene, announce that they and other Christians have decided to write down a statement, based on their faith, that challenges what's happening in the world around them. What could people of faith affirm in a situation like that?

Step 5 (five minutes). Asking the groups to "stay in character" as much as possible, invite the groups to think together about what Christians might say in such a setting. This step may be difficult for many. As soon as you sense a growing frustration or confused silence, move on to the next activity.

Step 6 (five minutes). Have the learners find the Declaration of Barmen in the *Book of Confessions.* (Note: You go over the structure of the Constitution more carefully in the following unit on polity.) Explain that this confession was written in precisely the situation they have been imagining. Call attention to the parts of the confession noted in the lesson plan that address the issue of who and what is Lord.

Step 7 (five minutes). Bring the small groups back together as a large group. Using references to the *Book of Order,* show how Presbyterians hold up the Lordship of Christ in what we believe.

- G-1.0100a—Jesus Christ is the Head of the Church. No human power or authority can claim our ultimate allegiance.

- G-1.0301(1)(a, b)—God alone is Lord of the conscience. The right of private discernment before God means we are accountable only to God for our beliefs.

- G-1.0302(2)—Corporate judgment also applies. While we are accountable ultimately to God alone for our beliefs, we have also agreed to be bound together as Presbyterians by shared understandings and commitments. This concept leads to the importance for Presbyterians of corporate deliberation and discernment of how God is speaking to today's Christians.

Step 8 (five minutes). Refer the learners to the paper *Hope in the Lord Jesus Christ*—or, if you don't have the full paper, refer to lines 155–168 only. Provide a brief background on the issues in the church that led to this paper. Call attention to lines 155–168 by reading and or displaying the text; invite discussion of how this way of stating the Lordship of Christ does or does not address the needs and concerns of today's Christians.

OFFICER DEVELOPMENT WORKSHOPS	Workshop #1	Theology
Jesus Christ is Lord	Time:	Date:

Objectives:

1. To welcome participants and introduce the course of study.
2. To introduce participants to the biblical and constitutional claim of the Lordship of Christ.
3. To invite participants to imagine their response to an external challenge to that Lordship.
4. To see how the church has actually responded to such a challenge (Declaration of Barmen).
5. To consider how belief in the Lordship of Christ might affect the way we live and have hope.

Duration (minutes)	Activity	Resources
10	**Step 1** **Welcome, Introductions, Housekeeping Details** • Review assignments from syllabus • Review use of study guide	Name tags and name tents (place cards) **Worksheet #1:** Workshop Overview and Assignments **Study Guide**
5	**Step 2** **Group Discussion—Worksheet #2** Were these difficult questions to answer? In what sense? Are these important questions? In what sense? Where do we look to find answers to these questions?	Worksheet #2: *Jesus Christ Is Lord*
3	**Step 3** **Romans 10:9—Mini-lecture** • Centrality of the text Used when members join Used when pastors, elders, deacons are ordained (G-14.0207) Used as charge at end of ordination (G-14.0209b) • The text itself Lord (*kurios* in Greek) → business, government, landowners, employers, slave masters, political officials, rulers—master, boss, Sir In NT, "Lord" is a title of honor reserved for Jesus the Christ—risen and glorified Frequently used in NT times to address the Roman emperor or in prayers to him Sharp contrast between secular lord and divine Lord	
2	**Step 4** **Guided Imagining** • You are one of a small group of Christians living during WWII in Germany • Together you have decided to write down a statement in reaction to what you see happening around you	

Duration (minutes)	Activity	Resources

5	**Step 5**
	Small-Group Reflection (around tables)
	  Ask: What are some of the things you think would be
	    important to say in a situation like we just
	    described?	

5	**Step 6** **The Declaration of Barmen** • Call folk together to hear how the church actually responded to such a situation • See *Book of Confessions* 8.11, 12, 15, 18, 21, 23, 24, 27	*Book of Confessions*

5	**Step 7**
	Mini-Lecture
	Jesus Christ is Head of the Church, G-1.0100a
	  no human power can claim our allegiance
	God alone is Lord of the Conscience, G-1.0301 (1)(a, b)
	Right of private discernment before God
	  Does this mean that it doesn't matter what we think or
	  believe? No!
	Corporate judgment also applies, G-1.0302 (2)
	  Theology of representation, deliberation, process,
	  committees!	

5	**Step 8**
	Jesus Christ—The Hope of the World
	  2000 Peacemaking Conference, Orange, California
	  • Rev. Dirk Ficca presented an address on living
	    faithfully in a diverse world
	  • In response to question, "How can a Christian live
	    out his or her own particular faith while being fully
	    engaged in a religiously plural world?" his answer,
	    opening the door to other ways of salvation, offended
	    many.
	  • The reaction across the church resulted in a paper
	    approved at the 214th GA entitled *Hope in the Lord
	    Jesus Christ*
	  • Read and/or display the text of lines 155–168
	  • Invite discussion on: How does this statement on the
	    Lordship of Christ address the needs of the church in
	    the modern, pluralistic world?
		Text to lines 155–168 of the paper *Hope in the Lord Jesus Christ* supplied as handout or written on flip chart or board

5	**Step 9** **Wrap-up, Questions, Responses** **Note:** the questions on worksheet #2, which we did earlier, were Questions 41, 38, and 40 of the *Study Catechism* (refer to www.pcusa.org)	Optional: copies of the *Study Catechism*
	Step 10 **End** (close with prayer)	

Step 9 (five minutes). Use the remaining time, if any, to respond to questions from the group. Before you conclude, you might announce that the questions on the worksheet that were so difficult to answer were, in fact, Questions #41, 38, and 40 of the *Study Catechism*.[4] Your learners will no doubt be interested in the church's answers to these questions.

Step 10. End this training session with a prayer for courage as the church lives out the Lordship of Christ. You want also to offer a blessing for the upcoming meal.

PART B: POLITY—CONSTITUTIONAL OVERVIEW AND PRESBYTERIAN PRINCIPLES

Step 1 (five minutes). Go over any additional housekeeping details that need addressing. If you have not done so already, make sure everyone knows to which small faith-sharing groups he or she is assigned. Participants stay with the same small groups every week for these faith-sharing experiences.

Step 2 (fifteen minutes). During this time, you lead the learners though a brief overview of the PC(USA) Constitution.

- Show the two books as Part 1 and Part 2. That Part 1 is the *Book of Confessions* is not without significance— theology comes before polity!

- Call attention to the table of contents in each book. Note the eleven confessions and three distinct sections of the *Book of Order*.

- Call attention to the numbering system used in both books.

- Make sure the learners know about the rather comprehensive index for each book. As a way of getting them used to perusing the index, have them look up the answer to the question, "What business can be transacted in a congregational meeting?"

- Note the special language for *permissive* and *mandatory* actions—explain the use of "shall," "should," "is appropriate," and "may."

- Invite learners to look up several references for practice. Use the suggestions on the lesson plan or use your own. Ask the question, then provide the citation to look up. Make sure everyone gets the hang of the numbering system.

OFFICER DEVELOPMENT WORKSHOPS	Workshop #1	Polity
Principles of Presbyterian Polity	Time:	Date:

Objectives:
1. To introduce participants to the Constitution of the PC(USA).
2. To introduce participants to the basic ideas that shape the Presbyterian Church.
3. To hear from participants what they like about being Presbyterian.

Duration (minutes)	Activity	Resources
5	**Housekeeping . . .** Cover any remaining issues, questions	
15	**Presentation** **Introduction to Constitution of PC(USA)** **Part 1**: *Book of Confessions* Eleven historic confessions **Part 2**: *Book of Order* Form of Government Directory for Worship Rules of Discipline **Numbering System**—see page in *BoO* facing table of contents **Index**—comprehensive index to content Question: What business can be transacted at a congregational meeting? (cite) **Language** (shall, should, is appropriate, may)—see preface **Lookup Practice**—have learners find the citations and answers to the following questions: [*BoC* 3.01] What do we acknowledge? [*BoC* 10.01 line 1] To whom do we belong? (note #10 even though there are eleven confessions) [G-10.0102(j)] The session is responsible for leading the congregation to what? [W-3.3616(d)] Who can serve Lord's Supper? [D-1.0102] What is the purpose of church power?	*Book of Order* *Book of Confessions*
10	**Small Groups** (around tables) Have learners share the responses on their worksheets	Worksheet #3: Principles of Presbyterian Polity
10	**Mini-Lecture** **The Presbyterian/Reformed Tradition** Provide brief overview using handout or your own content	Handout #1: Presbyterian/ Reformed Tradition
5	**What Is Good about Being Presbyterian?** Ask: What draws you to this particular way of thinking about, living out, and being the Church?	
	End with prayer	

Step 3 (ten minutes). Form small groups of four or five learners. Have each group compare their answers for Worksheet #3, "Principles of Presbyterian Polity." In the last few minutes, check in with the groups for any unresolved questions.

Step 4 (ten minutes). Reconvene the class as a whole. Using the material on Handout #1 ("Presbyterian/Reformed Tradition") or your own resources, provide a brief overview of the elements of the Reformed tradition. You may want to take a few minutes to explain where the term "Reformed" comes from and how it is connected to "Presbyterian."

Step 5 (five minutes). Find out how many of the participants grew up Presbyterian and how many chose to become Presbyterian. Invite the officers-elect to comment on what they find compelling about the Presbyterian way of doing things.

Step 6. Provide any instructions needed to move to the locations for the small groups for faith sharing.

Lesson Plan for Session 2

PART A: THEOLOGY—THE UNDERSTANDING AND USE OF HOLY SCRIPTURE

The material you are covering in this section has been problematic for the church for centuries. Most likely a wide spectrum of beliefs and opinions, some deeply held, exists on this topic. The leader is encouraged to lead with a confessional approach—stating as clearly as possible the confessional standards of the church while listening carefully to differing perspective.

Step 1 (ten minutes). This activity requires some movement around the room, so invite learners to store their books and move around. You need to set up the physical room to represent a continuum on which learners can stand to represent their position on a specific statement. Point to (or move to) one side of the room and declare it as the "Strongly Agree" side of the room. The opposite side is the "Strongly Disagree" side. The middle point in between represents the "I don't know/I am not sure/I don't care" place on the continuum. You do not have time to use all of the statements listed on the worksheet, so select five to seven as representative. Even add some of your own if you'd like.

The process goes like this. Read the statement out loud and invite the learners to position themselves physically on the continuum according to their response to the statement (strongly agree to strongly disagree or anywhere in between). Once folks have found their places, invite them to find one other person nearby (thus forming pairs), introduce themselves if unfamiliar, and provide a brief explanation as to why they are standing where they are standing.

A couple of rules are helpful.

- Arguing is not allowed. You may ask questions for clarification if needed. The goal is to understand the reasons behind a person's position.
- You may change your position on the continuum at any time you have new information or new understanding.

OFFICER DEVELOPMENT WORKSHOPS	Workshop #2	Theology
Understanding and Use of Holy Scripture	Time:	Date:

Objectives:
1. To hear from participants their views about Holy Scripture.
2. To introduce the Presbyterian/Reformed perspectives on Scripture.
3. To review Presbyterian guidelines for the understanding of and use of Scripture.

Duration (minutes)	Activity	Resources
10	**Here I Stand . . .** Using the physical space of the room as a continuum, declare one wall as Strongly Agree, the opposite wall Strongly Disagree, and the center space as the in-between. Invite participants to position themselves physically on the continuum in response to several statements chosen from the worksheet. After you read a statement and people are positioned, invite them to find one person close to where they are standing and explain why they are standing where they are standing.	**Worksheet #4:** The Bible Tells Me So
5	**Large Group** Briefly share your understanding of the Presbyterian/ Reformed position on several of the statements on the worksheet. (You will not have time to do them all.)	
10	**Mini-Lecture** The Bible in the Presbyterian/Reformed Tradition Review what the Confession of 1967 says about Scripture. Call attention to how the *Declaration of Faith* approaches the issues. Clarify its role as a study resource and not as a confessional document.	**Handout #2:** The Bible in Our Confessional Tradition
10	**Mini-Lecture** Review the guidelines developed over many years of struggle.	**Handout #3:** Presbyterian Guidelines for Scripture
10	**Wrap-up, Questions, and Responses** There will be questions!	
	End with prayer	

• Upon request, the leader indicates his or her own position on the continuum with regard to a particular statement.

Step 2 (five minutes). Invite folks back to their seats, and once again selecting representative statements, explain where the Presbyterian/Reformed tradition would stand on the continuum.

Step 3 (ten minutes). Distribute Handout #2: "The Bible in Our Confessional Tradition." Using the Confession of 1967, talk through how this confession understands Scripture and how it says we should use it. (Some analysts have said that the Confession of 1967 was the first confessional document of the Christian Church to affirm that the Bible needs to be interpreted.)

Also on the handout is a section from the Declaration of Faith, which is not an official confession but a study document that came out of the "southern stream" of the Church before reunion in 1983. Invite the learners to read the text, noting any surprises or points that need further explanation.

Step 4 (ten minutes). Distribute Handout #3: "Presbyterian Guidelines for Scripture" and present a mini-lecture on the specific guidelines that Presbyterians are invited to use in interpreting Scripture. (These guidelines came from two study papers—*Presbyterian Understanding and Use of Holy Scripture,* a position statement adopted by the 123rd General Assembly [1983] of the Presbyterian Church in the United States, and *Biblical Authority and Interpretation,* a resource document received by the 194th General Assembly [1982] of the United Presbyterian Church in the United States of America.)

Step 5 (ten minutes). Give yourself time to address questions that arise. Try to keep the focus on the confessional statements and the derived guidelines as the "official" Presbyterian position. This lesson offers a good opportunity to model forbearance with those who differ from each other and a time to remind the officers-elect about the tension between God alone being Lord of the individual's conscience and an officer's submission at times to the corporate judgment of the church.

Step 6. End with an appropriate prayer.

PART B: POLITY—THE SACRAMENTS/DIRECTORY FOR WORSHIP

The main part of this segment uses Worksheet #5: "Worship and Sacraments Quiz." Learners will have completed the quiz before class as one of their assignments for the workshop. Keep the tone light and try to have fun with the quiz. You might offer appropriate "prizes" for those who have a perfect score (or have a high score).

OFFICER DEVELOPMENT WORKSHOPS	Workshop #2	Polity
The Sacraments/Directory for Worship	Time:	Date:

Objectives:
  1. To review the Presbyterian/Reformed practice of and perspectives on the Sacraments.
  2. To introduce participants to the resources of the Directory of Worship.

Duration (minutes)	Activity	Resources
30	**Large Group** **Quiz Time** Review the questions and answers on the worksheet. See if there is a consensus for an answer from the group before you give the correct answer. Invite participants to cite references that support their answers. Use the questions to point out particular emphases of the Presbyterian/Reformed tradition and how they might differ from other Christian traditions (e.g., Roman Catholic, Episcopalian, Baptist)	**Worksheet #5:** Worship and Sacraments Quiz
5 church	**Small Groups** **The Elements of Worship** Invite table groups to identify in the order of worship those elements of worship listed in W-2.0, 2.1, 2.2, 2.3, 2.4, 2.5, 2.6	A copy of your bulletin/order of worship
5	**Mini-Lecture** The Directory for Worship Provide a brief overview of the content for the Directory for Worship, especially those aspects that were not raised in the answers to the quiz. Address how officers might use the Directory of Worship in their leadership roles.	*Book of Order*
5	**Wrap-up, Questions, Responses**	
	End with prayer	

Step 1 (thirty minutes). As you work through the questions, encourage the class to tell you what they think. Play with several ways for learners to indicate their responses. Get a show of hands for true and for false. Have them vote yea or nay. Vote with a show of hands.

After the "vote," ask for specific citations that provide a definitive answer. From time to time, ask individuals how they found that particular answer—what did they look up, and where?

Use the questions as opportunities to highlight the distinction between the Presbyterian/Reformed practices and beliefs and those of other denominations and traditions.

Step 2 (five minutes). Distribute copies of the bulletin from the previous Sunday's service. Invite the learners to form table groups of four or five persons to analyze the order of worship and identify any of the elements of worship (from W-2.0000–.6001) present in the order of worship.

Step 3 (five minutes). Provide a brief mini-lecture on the Directory of Worship, what it contains, and how it might be useful to officers and individuals for both private and corporate worship.

Step 4 (five minutes). Address any leftover questions or concerns from this or previous sessions. Record surplus questions for follow-up at a later time.

Step 5. End with an appropriate prayer.

Lesson Plan for Session 3

PART A: THEOLOGY—TO BE
OR NOT TO BE REFORMED

Learners will have completed Worksheet #6, "To Be or Not To Be Reformed," before the class, so you can jump right in. In this section, once again you deal with issues that are at best difficult and at worst divisive. For some officers-elect, this meeting will be the first time they have wrestled with theological issues from a Reformed perspective—a perspective that is, on occasion, at odds with popular religious belief. Be gentle in your explanations and focus always on the Scripture and our Confessions as the source and authority for our theology.

Step 1 (ten minutes). Ask folks to form groups of four or five persons. In their groups, they are to compare their opinions regarding the statements and viewpoints on the worksheet. Provide a two-minute warning before the time limit expires, and remind the groups to ensure everyone an opportunity to talk.

Step 2 (twenty minutes). Time will not be available during class to go over all the statements on the worksheet. Select a number of statements to address. Seek the collective wisdom of the whole class before you speak to the Presbyterian/Reformed perspective. For an example of how you might respond to a statement, see the second chapter of Rodger Nishioka's book, *The Roots of Who We Are,*[5] part of the Roots of Youth Ministry series, but equally valuable for adults as well.

After covering your selections, ask if there are any other items of particular interest to the class.

Step 3 (ten minutes). Using Handout #4, "Some Essential Tenets of the Reformed Tradition," or materials of your own choosing, present a mini-lecture or discussion on the essential tenets—where they are in the Constitution, whether there is a precise list, and how we "sincerely receive and adopt the essential tenets of the Reformed faith." You might want to provide some historical context—perhaps by noting that in the last seventy-five-plus years the church has steadfastly resisted attempts to be more specific about what is essential or to designate certain doctrines as a litmus test for orthodoxy. This opportunity is a great time, once again, to highlight the tension between matters of individual conscience and matters where the church has spoken (or in some cases avoided speaking).

Step 4 (five minutes). Wrap up any leftover questions and end with an appropriate prayer.

OFFICER DEVELOPMENT WORKSHOPS	Workshop #3	Theology
Presbyterian/Reformed Tradition Essential Tenets	Time:	Date:

Objectives:
1. To explore how the participants' beliefs compare to a Presbyterian/Reformed perspective.
2. To provide an overview of the distinctive beliefs of the Presbyterian/Reformed tradition.
3. To explore some of the essential tenets of faith as expressed in our Constitution.

Duration (minutes)	Activity	Resources
10	**Small Groups** **To Be or Not to Be . . .** Invite table groups to compare their responses to the worksheet.	Worksheet #6: To Be or Not to Be Reformed
20	**Large Group** **And the Answers Are . . .** Take an item on the worksheet and explain whether it is a 1, 2, or 3. Be prepared to point to specific references in the Constitution to support your contention. Note: You may not have time to cover all the items on the worksheet. Consider selecting several representative ones for more discussion. Leave some time for the participants to pose particular items of interest to them.	
10	**Mini-Lecture** **Some Essential Tenets** Using the handout or your own materials, provide an explanation of what the essential tenets are. Include your perspectives on the difference between an essential tenet and a litmus test or required subscription. Remind officers-elect about the tension between matters of conscience for individuals and the officer's submission to constitutional guidance.	Handout #4: Some Essential Tenets of the Reformed Tradition
5	**Wrap-up, Questions, Responses**	
	End with prayer	

PART B: POLITY—THE CONSTITUTIONAL QUESTIONS/DUTIES OF THE OFFICE

In this section, the officers-elect give careful thought to each individual question and assess the extent to which she or he can affirm it. They will have completed Worksheet #7, "Constitutional Questions," before coming to class.

Step 1 (ten minutes). Form groups of four or five people around tables. Ask each person to take one minute to share a constitutional question that received a high

OFFICER DEVELOPMENT WORKSHOPS	Workshop #3	Polity
Ordination Vows/Duties of the Office	Time:	Date:

Objectives:
1. To allow participants to reflect personally on the constitutional questions they will be asked and discuss their implications with others.
2. To review the duties for elders and deacons as listed in the *Book of Order.*

Duration (minutes)	Activity	Resources
10	**Small Groups** **The Constitutional Questions** Invite participants in their group: 1. To share in one minute one of the questions which for them was at the higher end of the scale (great enthusiasm) and some of the reasons that it was scored as such. 2. To share in one minute one of the questions which was for them lower than the others and some of the reasons that it was scored that way.	**Worksheet #7:** Constitution Questions
20	**Mini-Lecture** **The Constitutional Questions** Provide a brief commentary on each of the questions.	
10	**Mini-Lecture** **The Duties of the Office** Point out that in order to answer questions i. and j. in the affirmative, officers will need some idea of what their constitutional duties are. Review the duties for Elders (G-6.03) Deacons (G-6.04) Speak to the relationship between elders and deacons: what they have in common, and how they differ in function.	*Book of Order*
5	**Wrap-up, Questions, Responses**	
	End with prayer	

score (enthusiastic affirmation) and one minute to share a question that received a lower score (perhaps only relatively) than extremely enthusiastic. You may want to give a signal every two minutes so groups can move on to hear the next person.

Step 2 (twenty minutes). Provide a brief commentary on each of the constitutional questions. A great resource for this discussion is the little booklet *The Ordination Questions,* by Howard Rice and Calvin Chinn.[6] The cost is less than five dollars, making it an affordable resource for every officer-elect.

Step 3 (ten minutes). Shifting gears somewhat, but still presenting lots of information, lead the learners through a discussion on the duties of the office of elder and deacon as detailed in the *Book of Order*. Elder responsibilities can be found in G-6.03 and following. Duties for deacons can be found in G-6.04 and following. Note that the *Book of Order* references are generic to fit every congregation. Make sure you cover any duties or expectations of the office that are specific to your congregation. For example, if you have trustees, what are their duties? Are your deacons more pastoral in function or more likely to be in charge of buildings and grounds and finance? This section would be a good time to provide the meeting schedule for your governing bodies.

Step 4 (five minutes). Wrap up any loose ends or questions and end with an appropriate prayer.

Lesson Plan for Session 4

PART A: THEOLOGY—THE CONFESSIONS

For some, history is dry and boring. For others, history is the crucible that shapes and forms the present. Some have said that blood is on every page of the Confessions—blood wrought in the agony of wrestling with difficult issues, blood spilled by our ancestors who fought for what we now enjoy. To catch even a glimpse of that blood today can comfort us in our present struggles over theology, the interpretation of Scripture, and our identity as Presbyterian/Reformed Christians. Others have traveled these difficult roads successfully before us.

Theology does matter. We get our theology from Scripture—Scripture read through a particular lens called Presbyterian and Reformed. The Confessions bear witness to what is seen when we look through that lens. "They are the result of prayer, thought, and experience within a living tradition. They serve to strengthen personal commitment and the life and witness of the community of believers" (G-2.0500b).

Step 1 (five minutes). This day is the last meeting time for the workshops. A number of housekeeping details will need to be covered: schedules for upcoming events, encouraging learners to form "study groups" to collaborate on the study guide, identifying what other resources for further exploration are available (if not from your church, then from the Presbytery's Resource Center).

OFFICER DEVELOPMENT WORKSHOPS	Workshop #4	Theology
The Confessions	Time:	Date:

Objectives:
1. To explore the role of confessions in our church.
2. To acquaint participants with the eleven confessions of the PC(USA) and their time in history, geographical location, and some of the contextual issues the Confessions address.
3. To review and/or complete Worksheet #8.

Duration (minutes)	Activity	Resources
5	**Housekeeping** Because this workshop is the last, you may need to cover any questions about assignments or the schedule from here on.	
30	**Presentation** **The Confessions** Refer to appendix B for an outline of a presentation on the eleven confessions of the PC(USA). Respond to questions as they arise.	**Worksheet #8:** "Book of Confessions"
5	**Wrap-up, Questions, Responses** General questions on the Confessions	
5	**The Officer Examination** Give officers-elect an overview of what happens on the day of the exam. • Time, date, location • What they need to bring with them (two copies of their faith statement) • Who will be there • What will happen in the exam • Other information as necessary. (Covering this material before dinner will allow for further clarification over the meal if needed.)	
	End with prayer	

Step 2 (thirty minutes). Using the presentation outline included in appendix B or other resources, present a walk through *The Book of Confessions,* highlighting the time in history when each confession was written, where it was written, and what issues were being addressed in each confession. Although too long for use in this class setting (forty minutes), a great video overview on *The Book of Confessions* is available from Interlink Media Video Products (1-800-662-1151), titled *To All Generations* ($24.95). It would be quite useful in your preparations.

Encourage learners to confirm their responses and fill in any missing answers to the Worksheet #8: "The Book of Confessions."

Step 3 (five minutes). Invite questions or concerns about the confessional documents of the church.

Step 4 (five minutes). Take a few minutes before the meal to go over the details of the church officer examination by the session. Make sure everyone has the date, time, and location on their calendar. Remind them to bring two copies of their faith statement, one to turn in and one to keep for their files. (A guide for writing the faith statement is in appendix F.) Provide a brief overview of what will happen in the examination. If people need further clarification (as their anxiety rises), you can respond during the meal.

Step 5. End this section with a prayer, including the blessing for the meal.

PART B: POLITY—HOW YOUR CHURCH WORKS/HOW TO GET THINGS DONE

In this final section, you deal with the nuts and bolts of church work that are unique to your congregation. You need to think ahead about what is important for all the officers-elect to know and what things can be handled by printed materials, or perhaps a separate meeting. (See the section titled "Building a Team with Your Committee Chairs" in chapter 10.) You may want to include things that are important for both elders and deacons to know.

A strategy that requires a little more work is dividing the officers-elect into separate groups for elders and deacons and dealing with office-specific matters there.

Step 1 (two minutes). Start out the class by asking the learners to record on an index card two things—one thing that is really frustrating about working on church committees and one thing that is enjoyable about working on church committees.

Step 2 (three minutes). Quickly form groups of three (triads) and have each member share the two items on the index card.

Step 3 (five minutes). Have the pastor explain her or his expectations of officers in the church and what the officers can expect from the pastor(s) and staff.

Chat briefly about the church norms for taking a project or proposal from an idea to implementation.

- Can anyone recommend a project or identify a need?

- Do all ideas have to go through a committee? How does a person know which one?

- Can committees approve things, or do all things have to be approved by the session?

- Can a group raise money for their special project?

- Other questions

OFFICER DEVELOPMENT WORKSHOPS	Workshop #4	Polity
How your church works How to get things done	Time:	Date:

Objectives:
1. To orient church officers to ministry in your local congregation.
2. To explain the organizational structure of your church.
3. To explain where and how officers serve in that structure.
4. To have the pastor share his or her expectations regarding officers.

Duration (minutes)	Activity	Resources
2	**Individual** **Quick Survey** (written on index cards) Have each officer-elect write two things on an index card: 　1. one thing that's really frustrating about working on church committees 　2. one thing that he or she enjoys about working on church committees	
3	**Triads** (groups of three) **Quick Report** (one minute each) Have each member share their items with the others in their triad.	
5	**Mini-Presentation** **How Things Get Done in This Congregation** Provide a brief explanation of your own expectations and the church's norms for taking a project or proposal from idea stage to implementation.	
12	**Small Groups** **Organizational Review** Invite table groups to review the organizational information with an eye toward three questions: 　1. What general observations do you make about how this church is organized for ministry and mission? 　2. What seems to be areas of strength and areas of weakness? 　3. What else do you need to know?	Organizational lists or charts of your session and diaconate committees with names of committee leaders
10	**Questions and Answers** Invite all groups to report one question at a time.	
10	**Evaluation of Officer Development Workshops** Ask participants to reflect individually on their experience and to provide feedback for future planning.	Evaluation form or evaluation questions posted for all to see

Duration (minutes)	Activity	Resources
3	**Wrap-up, Closing Words** As you send the officers-elect off to their last small-group sharing time, consider offering • Appreciation for their participation • Excitement for the future • Additional help to those who might want it • Other sentiments or ideas	
	End with a prayer	

Step 4 (twelve minutes). Form groups of four or five persons around tables and provide each person with the organizational charts or committee lists for your congregation. Many officers-elect will be seeing these for the first time. Returning officers will view them through their past experiences. Invite the groups to review the information with special attention to these questions:

- What general observations can you make about how this church is organized for mission and ministry?

- What seem to be the strengths of our organization? What seem to be weaknesses?

- What other information would be helpful to you?

Step 5 (ten minutes). Leaving the groups where they are, ask for some feedback on the three questions. Make sure every group has had the opportunity to report something. You may want to record or compile the comments to pass on to whatever committee in your church deals with organizational issues.

Step 6 (ten minutes). Distribute an evaluation form. (Use the sample in appendix F or design your own.) Ask the officers-elect to provide honest feedback about their experience, any suggestions they have for improvement the next time, and insights into what the experience has meant for them personally.

Step 7 (three minutes). Wrap up this section and the entire series of workshops by expressing your appreciation to the officers-elect for their willingness to serve, for the time they have invested in preparation for service, and for the hope you have for the future of the church under their leadership. Offer any reminders or last-minute logistical concerns and end with an appropriate prayer.

Possible Topics for Teaching

Below are a few topics in theology and polity that could be included in an officer training session. Some have been included in the sessions described earlier in this chapter, but others have not.

Theology

- Jesus Christ is Lord

- Authority of Scripture

- Confessions (part 1 of the constitution)

- Essential tenets, diversity, "Always Being Reformed"

- Sovereignty of God, sinfulness of humans

- Salvation by grace alone

- Election for service and salvation (horizontal and vertical faith)

- The covenant life (discipline and order) and stewardship (management)

- Idolatry and tyranny—justice and obedience

Polity

- The PC(USA) Constitution/*Book of Order* (part 2 of the constitution)

- Directory for Worship/Sacraments

- Ordination vows

- Duties of elders/deacons

- How your church works to fulfill those duties

- Historic principles of church order

- The Great Ends of the Church

- Church discipline

- Comparison of three polities—congregational, Presbyterian, Episcopal

Chapter 7

Sharing Personal Faith
in Small Groups

In the Presbyterian Church (U.S.A.), we examine people as to their personal faith to make sure that our leadership has this quality. For us, faith is personal, but never private. John Calvin wrote:

> [T]he Gospel is not a doctrine of the tongue but of life. It cannot be grasped by reason and memory only but is fully understood when it possesses the whole soul and penetrates to the inner recesses of the heart. . . . [o]ur religion will be unprofitable, if it does not change our heart, pervade our manners, and transform us into new creatures.[1]

Small groups are an excellent way for officers to share their faith perspectives. After all, Jesus was a small-group leader! He nurtured his students in a small group. They shared meals together, prayed together, studied together, and experienced hardships together. The Christian faith has always been cultivated in relationships. In that sense, it is incarnational.

Although the particular small groups formed for the training sessions will only be together as a group for four meetings, they will spend three years together serving on the session or diaconate. The relationships kindled within these groups will literally last a lifetime. Read some of the comments in the conclusion of this book, and you can see how valuable these little groups are.

Neil McBride wrote a book titled *How to Lead Small Groups*, wherein he identifies several practical principles concerning small-group development.[2] Of these, five in particular relate to the type of small groups that are formed during the training sessions:

• People prefer to participate in groups where other members are similar in age, attractiveness, attitudes, personality, economic status, perceived ability, and needs. (McBride's Principle 3)

• The smaller the group, the greater the feasibility of shared leadership. (McBride's Principle 6)

• The physical setting in which the group meets affects members' attitudes and actions and, consequently, helps determine group process. (McBride's Principle 7)

• Members are more highly motivated and perform more efficiently when the group possesses clear goals and an understanding of what must be done to accomplish goals. (McBride's Principle 11)

• Groups whose members are heterogeneous with respect to sex and personality types are more conforming and perform more effectively than groups that are homogenous with respect to characteristics. The opposite is true for age. Diversity among the members in some areas is helpful to the group's success. (McBride's Principle 14)

In our church, we divide the deacons into groups and the elders into groups and intentionally preselect who will be in which group. When we do that, we consider things like:

• Separating close friends

• Mixing up ages

• Balance of men and women

• Balance of old guard/new guard

• Balance of conservatives/liberals (Make sure you have some of each!)

We intentionally put people with others whom they may not know in order to build respect and stronger ties within groups.

Clergy are excluded from the groups. There's no leader or facilitator. We usually ask the youngest person in the group (they have to discover who that is) to be the timekeeper. It's a group of equals.

Each group works best with six members, and probably would not work well at all with less than four. Some smaller churches may only have a single group of four or five. That's okay. When you are only training three or four elders (in a unicameral system), consider joint training with other small churches or a cluster of churches.

Because the groups only have forty-five minutes each week to share, the process is designed to maximize time together. You can aid this by assigning each group to a separate room in the church that will be their room for all four training sessions. Note that membership in each small group remains the same from session to session. This arrangement builds trust and unity at the expense of not getting to know the others quite as well. It's a trade-off, but one that is worthwhile.

Each week, the class receives a worksheet to complete ahead of time for next week's small-group meeting. The worksheets are handed out at the orientation meeting. Insist that the participants write out their responses ahead of time and not just make up their response during the meeting. Thought-out responses are much better. (See appendix E for the worksheets that we use.)

Chapter 8

Officer Examination

Once you have completed the officer training sessions, you need to set the date for the session's examination of the officers-elect. The process we are suggesting can be done as part of a regular session meeting or as a separate meeting for just the examination.

Ideally, though not necessary, the whole session is involved in the examination. The *Book of Order* (G-9.0502) provides for a minimum of two elders and one permanently installed clergy person to be designated as a commission of the session to examine the officers-elect. Whether done by a commission or the whole session, minutes noting the names of those examined, their completion of a period of study, and the approval of the examination should be recorded (G-14.0205).

We have found that a one-on-one examination can be intimidating for all involved. Our suggestion is to have two or three elders examine a group of two or three officers-elect. One of the elders is designated the "table moderator" and is responsible for managing that group's examination.

Sometimes securing enough elders to have two or three per group of officers-elect may be difficult. In these cases, recruiting elders who are not in active service to assist in the examination can be helpful. Often, elders report that being involved in the examination process is a high point for them, whether currently serving on the session or not in active service. They also express appreciation for being reminded of the things that make us Presbyterian as they hear responses from the officers-elect.

If you do use elders not in active service, make sure you still have the proper number of active elders for the examination to be official—in the case using the whole session, a quorum; in the case of the commission, the minimum number of elders and clergy.

We also recommend having a meal together before the examination. The meal serves several purposes. Presbyterians are always pleased to gather around a table. In this informal fellowship setting, previous and current elders can get to know the officers-elect over table conversations. The meal provides a time buffer so that folks who may be running late do not interrupt an examination already in progress. Enjoying a meal together also helps to reduce (though not completely) the anxiety many officers-elect experience prior to the examination. You may want to consider making the officers-elect guests for the meal at the church's expense as a way of saying thanks for all the hard work of preparation and their willingness to serve the congregation as an officer.

Preparations for the Exam

Prior to the time of the examination, a number of things must be done.

• Set the date and time of the exam very early in the process (even before the nominating committee develops a slate of officers) so that everyone can schedule it on their calendars.

• You may want to schedule a make-up date to handle the inevitable schedule conflicts. You can use this opportunity for a session commission to examine a smaller number of people.

• Make arrangements for the meal, if there is to be one.

• Based on the number of officers-elect to be examined, recruit the needed number of table moderators and other elders to conduct the exam.

• Provide reminders to all involved regarding date, time, location, cost of meal, expectations, and any other logistical issues. (See the sample letters to elders, officers-elect, and table moderators in appendix F. The memo to table moderators includes some practical advice for common situations.)

• Provide the examining elders with a copy of the study guide (appendix A) with answers. Note: The elders preparing for the examination often reinforce their own knowledge of the areas covered in the exam—a significant plus for everyone.

• Give some thought to assigned seating for both the elders and the officers-elect. Provide a mix of male-female, seasoned-novice, and introvert-extrovert elders at each table.

The Faith Statement

As part of preparing for the examination, each officer-elect develops a statement of faith to be read and shared as the first part of the examination. The faith statement is one concrete way for elders to know something of the personal faith of each officer-elect.

If the officers-elect have not done such a thing before, provide some guidance prior to the examination. Guidelines for writing a faith statement are included as a handout in appendix F.

We ask each person being examined to bring two copies of their faith statement with them to the examination: one to turn in and one to keep for their files. The faith statements are kept on file with the pastor(s) and are not otherwise distributed. As one way of helping officers-elect understand the faith statement, consider making available several diverse examples from previous examinations or settings (removing names and other identifying information).

As officers-elect develop their faith statement, remind them:

- A faith statement is not a telling of their faith journey ("I grew up in a Christian home"), but rather more like a "confession" articulating what he or she believes as a person of faith.

- A faith statement is often in the form of "I believe. . . ."

- A faith statement can be expressed in different forms (narrative and poetry are common).

- A faith statement often includes specific statements of belief in (but not limited to) the following areas:

  ○ God

  ○ Jesus Christ

  ○ The Holy Spirit

  ○ The Bible

  ○ The Church

  ○ One's sense of call, purpose, or mission in the world.

Because faith statements are by nature personal and subjective, evaluation of them is not on a right-or-wrong basis. Each faith statement is a gift from the officer-elect. Nevertheless, having said that, at the time of the examination, table moderators and examining elders may determine that a particular faith statement is deficient if little thought went into it or it is clearly more a telling of a faith journey (biography and history) rather than a statement of what the person believes. In such situations, asking the officer-elect to rewrite the statement may be appropriate.

The Examination—Step-by-Step

If you are having a meal (recommended), allow thirty to forty-five minutes for eating and time for fellowship around the table.

At the appointed time for the exam, convene the session or commission with prayer and any instructions that might be necessary. Remind all involved of the sequence of events and what is expected. Remind them that the table moderators guide the process. If you are using the suggested grouping (two or three elders with two or three officers-elect), the examination will take about forty-five minutes.

The first task is for the officers-elect to share their statements of faith. This time is not for debate or discussion, but a time to receive with appreciation this expression of personal faith. Questions for clarification or requests for elaboration are appropriate.

The table moderator may additionally choose some or all of the questions in section one of the study guide dealing with personal faith. Ask each question of each officer-elect in turn. Once all the officers-elect at the table have shared their statements of faith and responded to other questions in the area of personal faith, move to the next phase of the exam.

At this point the table moderator becomes the guide through the examination in the prescribed content areas: knowledge of the doctrine, government, and discipline contained in the constitution of the church, and the duties of the office (G-14.0205).

The study guide is divided into sections based on these content areas. The table moderator generally introduces a new content area with a question chosen from that section. Other elders at the table may also pose questions from the study guide. The table moderator watches the clock and keeps the process moving to conclude within the time allowed.

In this model, the officers-elect are permitted to bring with them to the examination their copy of the study guide and the answers they have made to the questions. In one sense, this is an "open book" examination. The examinees may refer to their notes, as no one expects them to have memorized all the information.

However, the officers-elect are expected to be familiar enough with the material to use their own words and not read verbatim from their notes.

The study guide is just that: a guide for examiners and examinees. Examining elders may come up with their own questions, but they are encouraged to avoid esoteric areas where even die-hard Presbyterians fear to tread.

Questions should be addressed to specific officers-elect with the encouragement for other officers-elect to add their additional comments or responses. Table moderators need to ensure that one knowledgeable or gregarious officer-elect doesn't monopolize the answer time to the exclusion of the other examinees.

Five minutes or so before the end of the allotted time, provide an appropriate five-minute warning so the table moderators can wrap up the examination.

When time is up, give everyone a break. During this time, meet with the table moderators to determine any concerns regarding any officer-elect being inadequately prepared to serve as a church officer.

While approving everyone's examination may seem the "Christian" thing to do, moderators should use the time to guarantee the integrity of the whole process of preparation for service. When might it be appropriate to question the readiness of an officer-elect to serve? While each individual examination will vary, every officer-elect is expected to prepare, at least minimally, for the examination. If a person simply and clearly did not bother to prepare—perhaps trusting that he or she would not be held accountable for this lack of preparation—then now is the time to question his or her readiness to serve. The high expectations of this model of church officer development will be difficult to maintain in the future if word gets out that preparation is unimportant.

Some situations may arise where it becomes apparent that an officer-elect cannot affirm some "essential tenet" (for instance, does not believe in infant baptism, or denies the sovereignty of God) or is unable to answer all ordination questions affirmatively.

In both of theses cases, suspend for a time the examination of the individuals in question and do not take immediate action on their examination. While certainly awkward, doing so would give some needed time for members of the session (or its commissioned subgroup) to confer privately with the officers-elect to raise concerns and determine appropriate actions. This approach would also provide a public witness to the session's intention to maintain the integrity of the preparation and examination process.

The possibility of such an event taking place suggests that the examination date should be scheduled several days or weeks in advance of the service where new elders and deacons are to be ordained and installed to provide adequate time to address any needed delays.

After the table moderators have conferred and the session (or commission) is reconvened, a motion to approve the examination of the officers-elect is in order. Having been approved, the officers-elect can be welcomed. If the examination is done by a commission of the session, their work concludes with prayer as normal. If the examination is a part of a session meeting, the session may invite the officers-elect to stay for the meeting.

Following the model established in the worship segments of the officer development workshops, a brief worship and Communion service should be included as part of the examination. Depending on your pattern for such services, worship and Communion could take place immediately following the vote approving the examination or as the last item on the session agenda before adjournment. In either case, celebrating the Lord's Supper together can be a powerful witness to the grace that will support your common ministry in the years to come. Some groups find that participating in Communion while standing in a circle further reinforces their sense of shared ministry.

Chapter 9

Moving Away from "Bored" Meetings

Once you've trained new officers in such a fashion, the last thing you want to do is throw them into a "bored" meeting. They will be fed, motivated, stimulated, and ready to go. Imagine their first session meeting or their first deacons' meeting. It could kill all the good work you've done. Ed White, senior consultant with the Alban Institute in Washington, D.C., helped us get away from "bored" meetings at Mount Pleasant Presbyterian Church. His suggestions carried over to Myers Park. We basically did away with the agenda!

The change actually had its roots in the training sessions. A group of new officers wondered why we did not have worship at our regular meetings. (You gotta love that!) So, we added a thirty-minute worship service to the meeting schedule, following the model used in training. One can't just add thirty minutes to an already full meeting, though—and even adding worship did not address other problems with the way our meetings were structured.

Our committees came to "report" to the session, which in effect turned our leaders into managers. No one was leading the church; we were just listening to reports on where it's been. The only thing left to do was micromanage, so we would have an hour of discussion on whether we should hang a portrait of a former pastor in the Fellowship Hall or the parlor. Maybe the chapel would be better, or even the library. "No, we can't hang that portrait because we don't have portraits of all the other former pastors." "OK, so who will be in charge of getting those?" "Do we have to pay for them to have portraits made? If so, that's not in the budget." Our meetings devolved into such discussions on far too many occasions.

At our annual officers' retreat, Ed White suggested to us that the format of having committees report to the session and diaconate was outdated. We must have picked this model up from corporate America, United Way, or *Robert's Rules of Order*. Ed suggested that we send it back!

Ed further suggested a pivotal change: having just one area of our ministry come to the session each meeting. This approach allows time for the leadership to wrap its arms fully around one aspect of the church. By doing so, the session learns what's going on and has an opportunity to provide input. We even have time to pray with the folks who are doing that ministry! Here is a sample of our schedule:

Session Meetings for 2003

January	Outreach
February	Education
March	Worship
April	Officer exam (joint meeting with diaconate)
May	Denominational relations (General Assembly issues, inquirers/candidates, presbytery issues, etc.)
June	Stewardship
July	No meeting
August	Budget (We go through the budget process in April/May)
September	Evaluation and long-range planning
October	Pastoral care, diaconate
November	Youth
December	Open meeting

Under this new format, the council and committee members also join the session for dinner and worship (dinner from 5:30 to 6:30 p.m. before worship), which has proven to be a valuable bonding experience. The groups who join us leave feeling appreciated, prayed for, supported, encouraged, challenged, and hopeful. Isn't that what leadership should be doing for the church?

In order to free up the session to do this work, we had to empower committees. We researched the *Book of Order* to determine what a session actually had to vote on and we discovered only six items:

1. Electing elders to serve as commissioners to presbytery and electing the treasurer and clerk

2. Approving the budget

3. Membership matters (receive, transfers, deletions, etc.)

4. Calling congregational meetings

5. Approving examinations of elders and deacons

6. Worship matters, including baptisms and the Lord's Supper

Everything else can be delegated and supervised. The session doesn't lose any power. It still has the authority to redirect a committee, to charge a group with a task, and to guide and direct the overall ministry of the church.

This empowerment through the committees requires a significant amount of trust as well as effective communication. The alternative is to keep committees under thumb. To do so, however, limits growth and wastes leadership. We charged each committee to do its work within the parameter of its job description and budget. They love it, and it works beautifully.

We also charged the committees to be accountable. Each month, every committee provides the clerk with a one-page report in two parts: FYI and Action Items. The FYI comes in bullet fashion. Do not allow committees to simply submit their minutes. By putting their items in bullet points, committees have to summarize their work and list only what is valuable for the session to know. We have very few Action Items. However, the session can pull any FYI item off the list for discussion and possible redirection, thus keeping the session in the leadership seat.

The good news about this empowerment model is that it frees the session to provide leadership to the various ministries of the church and alleviates micromanaging. This model puts trust in our committees and supports the work of ministry. We leave the meetings uplifted and not downtrodden.

Sometimes you may have to adjust the schedule. Items come up that need the session's full attention. Be flexible, and you can make it work. For example, we once had to cancel a group's scheduled time with the session, which necessitated rescheduling them for a later month, when they had to split the time with the group originally scheduled for that time period. The solution was not ideal, but it worked.

You need to spend a fair amount of energy educating your committee people as to their new freedoms and responsibilities. They will need help preparing the first few monthly reports and also in putting together their first meeting with the session.

Ultimately, this approach can lead to some exciting and innovative exchanges between your session and your committees. We have certainly had some creative evenings. The outreach council at Myers Park loaded up the session and drove them down to Urban Ministries in uptown Charlotte, North Carolina. We had Communion in the old train station where countless homeless people come for help each day. Two of those homeless people met with us and shared their experience of living on the streets. None of us have forgotten the experience. How do you think that might affect us the next time we are setting the budget?

The worship council led the session in designing its worship service for the evening, a powerful service in which everyone participated. We learned a lot about our responsibilities to provide worship for the congregation.

The education council engaged the session in true education format. We had PowerPoint displays, surveys, focus groups, presentations, and handouts. The group gleaned from the session its concerns about our educational ministry and took suggestions back to hammer out new plans.

Our denominational relations committee invited Dr. Tom Currie, dean of Union-PSCE at Charlotte, to share with us the exciting work of our new seminary extension. Tom brought one of his students, Lori Raible, who will soon be an inquirer for our church. One of our pastors, who had attended last year's General Assembly, provided a PowerPoint presentation on the role and work of the General Assembly. (It just so happened that the assembly was meeting at the same time as this presentation.) We discussed some of the issues that were before the General Assembly this year. The committee wrapped up its time with a brief update on the work of our presbytery and synod. It was a very enlightening presentation.

Our long-range planning committee currently intends to have the session read Anthony B. Robinson's *Transforming Congregational Culture*[1] in preparation for their time with the session next fall. They will have a panel discussion with three age groups: young adult, middle-age, and older adults, with five members in each group. The focus of the readings and the discussion is to help the session begin to identify needs for ministry in order to strategically plan for the future. What a great idea!

This type of meeting format is a creative process. It stimulates all of our leaders in the church, not just the session. Each council has reported positive feedback and a renewed sense of energy for its task. Isn't this what leadership should be doing for the church?

The changes did not stop with the session and its extensions, however. Our deacons were reorganized to be pastoral care providers. They no longer look after buildings, but people. Consequently, the deacons have very little on which to vote.

The *Robert's Rules of Order* mode of meeting made absolutely no sense for our deacons, so we moved away from it.

The deacons also have a meal together followed by worship/Communion in the sanctuary. They then go to the Fellowship Hall and have an inspirational speaker for the evening. We started putting something back into our deacons to support them in their care-giving ministries. It works!

After the first year of having a theme for the night, you might consider going every other month and having the off months open for general business of the session. This schedule helps avoid burning out on the themes and gives the session opportunities to address various concerns that need attention.

You get the general idea. We have moved away from "bored" meetings, and the leaders have retained, if not enhanced, their leadership function. We empowered committees to do their work, which is all accountable and supported. We are spending time with those who are doing the work of the church. The leaders are leading. Isn't that what leadership is supposed to do?

Chapter 10

Other Team-Building Opportunities

If we train officers and then turn them loose to serve out their term, we will reap what we sow. The job doesn't stop with training. It *starts* with training. There's an old saying, "You can't change the past, but you can change the future." To strengthen a congregation for the future requires a systemic approach to developing leaders. Checking off a training program from the church's to-do list won't cut the mustard. Leadership development must permeate everything we do.

Staff Meetings

Staff meetings are typically about as enjoyable as changing a flat tire . . . on the interstate . . . at night . . . in the rain. You catch my drift! Here's another place to change the way we do business.

Most of our churches have a very small staff. In my first church, it was just me. I ran the bulletin and newsletter, answered the phone, preached the sermons, buried the dead, baptized the new, married couples, taught classes, cleaned toilets, and did anything else that needed doing. Plenty of people are in that situation. A pastor in such a church must rely on the members to share in the work of ministry.

An extremely small staff has a difficult time doing any group work. Even in large churches, program staff and support staff are divided. Sometimes they speak different languages. A pastor, a secretary, and a sexton could be a team, but the dynamics are surely different from those of large staff configurations. Given the staff variations, if you have a group large enough to do some team building, consider some of the following suggestions.

We moved our staff meetings to the sanctuary in the same manner that we shifted the session and diaconate meetings to begin in that significant setting. Our staff also worships together. We don't celebrate Communion together, but we follow a similar format as that of the session and diaconate. The move to the sanctuary does something. In that room we take our baptism vows, worship, celebrate Communion, exchange wedding vows, pray, sing, conduct funerals, and give our money, our hearts, and our lives to God. The sanctuary is a powerful room for a staff meeting.

After worship, we divide our staff into smaller teams: outreach, education, worship, sextons, business office, and so on. Each team includes clergy, program staff, and administrative assistants related to that ministry area. Thirty minutes is allowed for the teams to meet. Following team meetings, the program staffs meet for thirty minutes to clear all calendar events and do a little think-tank work.

Our final meeting is the clergy team. We go over worship details for Sunday and pastoral care concerns. We also check schedules and discuss weddings, baptisms, funerals, and whatever else is left.

The schedule looks like this:

9:30–10:00 a.m.	Worship
10:00–10:30 a.m.	Teams
10:30–11:00 a.m.	Program staff
11:00–11:30 a.m.	Clergy

By using this model, people are not wasting their time sitting in a meeting with an agenda that doesn't relate to their ministry area. The groups keep changing locations, so the energy usually stays with us.

We have a large staff. You may glean some ideas from our format and adapt them to your situation. Smaller staffs can worship together and find ways to meet in cluster groups that share related work.

Building a Team with Your Committee Chairs

Because covering in the four workshops all the things an officer needs to know in order to serve in a particular congregation effectively is not possible, you may find it helpful to provide an additional learning opportunity for those installed officers who serve as committee chairs or vice-chairs.

Some churches have a rotation system in place wherein a vice-chair is expected to serve as the chair of the committee when the current chair rotates out of the leadership position. In some settings, cochairs follow a similar pattern. Some congregations may use different terminology for the leadership roles and for their organizational structure. In this section, the use of the term "chair" includes cochair, vice-chair, or any other designated leadership role within the church. The use of the term "committee" also includes councils, work groups, departments, ministry teams, and so on when referring to a designated group within a church's organizational structure. In short, the folks who need to attend this recommended workshop are any persons serving in any leadership capacity on the governing boards of your church, plus any other leaders who might benefit from the information presented in this workshop.

The purpose of this supplemental workshop for committee leaders is to provide them with the nuts-and-bolts information needed to understand and work effectively in your particular congregation.

Some of the things you might consider covering in this workshop are:

- Suggestions for how to use committee meetings to nurture the spiritual growth of its members in addition to completing tasks

- Resources for use in committee devotional time

- Ways to do team building for ministry

- Your church's stated mission, vision, or purpose and how a particular committee fits into the larger plan

- Your pastor's vision for the coming months and years

- Your pastor's expectations for church officers and what officers can expect from her or him

- How your congregation is organized for mission (organizational charts, committee member lists/directories, staff charts, who's responsible for what, etc.)

- Job descriptions for committees; when and how often do they meet?

- How is information relayed from committees to the supervising governing body (minutes, verbal reports, staff liaisons, etc.)?

- What are the expectations for committee record-keeping? (format; content: journal of meeting or summary of items for information and items for action; who gets them? by when?)

- Importance of recording in the minutes any approvals for disbursement of committee-authorized funds

- How to request and/or authorize a check from the church

- Financial accounting norms and policies

- How to read and understand a typical church financial statement

- How to find out how much money your committee has spent/remaining for this year

- How the church financial accounts are organized (operating funds, endowments, restricted funds, etc.)

- How annual budgets are developed and the committee's role and responsibility in that process

- How to schedule an event on the church calendar and request a particular room set-up

- How officers and committees are involved in the overall stewardship emphasis in the church

- How officers are involved in the annual financial stewardship campaign

- How to get publicity in the church bulletin/newsletter/on bulletin boards (What are the deadlines for publicity?)

- How church staff relates to the committee

- Can a church secretary take minutes for meetings?

- How do chairs and committees get copies made?

- What are the church's policies and procedures?

- Who do chairs and committees go to for questions?

- How can chairs run a better committee meeting?

- How can chairs stop certain people from frustrating every meeting they attend?

- What resources are available to support the work of committee leaders, and how are they accessed?

- Who are the members of this church and how can they be contacted? (An up-to-date church directory is the easiest way to respond to this question.)

This list is just a representative sample of nuts-and-bolts issues for many church leaders. No doubt you can add many more from your church's history and experience. Every church is different, but this list is a good starting point.

For most churches, the list will be quite daunting. You may wonder how you will ever get that much information across in the time that most committee leaders have to give for that purpose. The simple answer is: you can't. Instead of filling your leader's brains with the answers to these and other questions, a better approach may be to teach how to find the information when the leaders need it.

This approach requires a lot of preparation. Information needs to be written down in order to be readily accessible to others. If your church has a strong oral tradition of passing on such information verbally, several years may be needed to compile all the bits and pieces of your policies and procedures into a coherent whole.

Having answers to your list of questions compiled into some sort of committee leader's handbook, however, contributes to effective and productive ministry in the present and for years to come. Just avoiding the frustration that comes from each new committee leader having to learn how your church works through trial and error—and finally "getting it" only months before he or she rotates off the committee—makes the effort worthwhile.

Whether you have all your answers written down or not, meeting with all committee chairs together is likely to be helpful. You may have to have two or more meetings to accommodate the scheduling needs of your committee chairs. In addition to providing an opportunity to do some team building among those who are directly responsible for carrying out your church's ministries, this meeting is also an opportunity to put the same information out to everyone at the same time, and to answer questions once instead of multiple times.

Planning a Committee Leaders' Meeting

The specific content for a committee leaders' meeting useful for your particular congregation will be unique to your setting. Here are some ideas, though, to get you started.

• Several months in advance of the meeting, gather your planning committee—or two or three persons connected to the organizational structure of the church (clerk of session, previous committee chairs, etc.)—to brainstorm a list of topics that committee leaders need to know. Use the above list to start, and add any items unique to your setting.

• Go back over the list and place the items in categories:

  ○ Information that can be communicated easily on paper (schedules, policies, deadlines, etc.). Use this category to determine what paper resources need to be accumulated and prepared for distribution.

  ○ Information that can be communicated on paper but needs further explanation (financial statements, certain policies, organizational structure, etc.). Line up presenters from the church leaders and staff for each item.

  ○ Skills that need developed (e.g., how to run better meetings). Think about who in the church or local area could facilitate such a skill development segment.

  ○ Areas where motivation or inspiration are needed (e.g., hopes and dreams for the next five years). The pastor or perhaps an outside speaker could do this.

  ○ Areas that require group reflection or interaction (Bible study on leadership, evaluation of current programs, strategic planning for the future). Who can facilitate these needs?

• Once you have the items in these or other categories, go back over the list and estimate how long each item will take. A three-hour workshop is a reasonable time frame for this kind of meeting.

• If, as is likely the case, you have more material to cover than time will allow, prioritize the list in terms of importance for your needs. You may want to think about which items will benefit from being handled in a gathering of leaders and which can be handled by each leader individually. (Note: Printed resources, if assembled beforehand in a committee leader's notebook, may not require lengthy explanation and can serve as an ongoing resource for committee leaders.)

• Line up presenters and speakers.

• Create an agenda for the workshop.

• Publicize how committee leaders will benefit from attending.

- Prepare in advance all materials for distribution.

- Make the meeting location as comfortable as possible, and provide refreshments.

- Take a few minutes at the end of your meeting for committee leaders to fill out a brief evaluation form with some general questions, such as these:

  ○ What aspects of this workshop were helpful to you?

  ○ What aspects of this workshop were not helpful?

  ○ (For follow-up) What did you need that wasn't covered?

  ○ What would you suggest be done differently next time?

  ○ Do you have any other words of wisdom for next year's meeting planners?

If you fall into a pattern of yearly committee leaders' meetings, you may want to consider dividing your workshop at some point into two tracks: one for new committee leaders and one for continuing leaders who probably won't want to repeat basic information covered in a previous year's workshop.

The College of Elders

There's nothing in the *Book of Order* about a college of elders. I am not even sure where the idea came from, but it was from another Presbyterian Church (U.S.A.) congregation. The idea is to maintain a relationship with all elders of your church.

The college of elders has no power. It cannot set policy, vote, endorse, change anything, or prevent anything. Every living elder in your church belongs to the college of elders. Don't forget those elders who have transferred into your church from another PC(USA) church. "Once an elder, always an elder."

We have an annual banquet for the college of elders. That's the only meeting they have, and it's a very special evening. We have a great meal, a little entertainment, and a brief presentation. Our youth often serve as waiters/waitresses for the banquet. We acknowledge our oldest and youngest elder and the class just recently elected. We mention any elders who have transferred out or died since our last meeting. We also welcome new elders who have recently joined the church. It's a team-building night!

The presentation varies, but it is always upbeat and informative. We want our leadership to know what's going on in the church. Upcoming capital campaigns, new ventures, and future projects are all excellent examples of presentation topics. The bottom line is to keep the leadership informed and feeling like they belong to the team. How many elders have said, "Once I got off the session, I was out of the loop"? The college of elders eliminates this problem.

We also give the elders an opportunity to sign up for various ministries within the church. We have sign-up tables all around the room. They can sign up to be lay readers, act as elder greeters, serve home-bound Communion, be on a specific task force, substitute teach, go on a mission trip, attend presbytery meetings, and so forth. These tasks are all great ways to utilize your elders while they are off the session. They appreciate being asked. These are your leaders. Keep them stimulated.

The Annual Leadership Retreat

Every winter we have our annual leadership retreat. We bring in a facilitator and meet on Friday evening and Saturday morning. Each year, we select a different focus for the retreat. Deacons, elders, and program staff (including clergy) attend the retreat. Friday evening is usually off-site, but in town. We have used museums, neighborhood clubhouses, hotel conference rooms, and so on. The off-site setting moves us out of the church and into the community. It's a way to be church without the buildings, and it works. We always share a meal together, followed by the evening presentation. Saturday we meet in our Fellowship Hall with a continental breakfast, followed by a presentation and workshops, and we conclude with lunch. Friday has been more of a lecture/dialogue format, while Saturday utilizes small groups, mini-lectures, and a seminar format.

We elect elders and deacons at our January annual congregational meeting. The new class is expected to attend the retreat even before they have completed their training. It helps build the team. The exiting class (we rotate in June) also attends. We use the time to thank them for their years of service and inform them of their new upcoming role in the college of elders. We also invite any committee chairs and vice-chairs who may not be deacons or elders.

Our facilitators have been pastors in churches similar to our size or larger. We have also used folks like Ed White, senior consultant with the Alban Institute in Washington, D.C. You need to consider the areas of need in your congregation and seek out leaders in those areas. Stay away from always having a topic on strategic planning, finances, long-range planning, and the like. Consider having the retreat on prayer or Bible study. Leaders need spiritual development. A spiritual life retreat reaps big benefits. We have also had our leadership read a book together and then invited the author to be our retreat leader. Not all writers are retreat leaders, but with some pre-thought this experience can be a rich one.

Both the college of elders and the annual leadership retreat create a fellowship for our leaders. They get fed so they can feed. They enjoy each other. These people have similar levels of commitment to Christ and to his Church, and can grow to love one another with the right opportunity to do so. This fellowship helps their work as a leadership team later on as well; it's difficult to bite someone at a subsequent meeting when you've grown to love them. (I think Jesus said something like that.) Anyway, it works.

Continuing Education Options

Even if your officers-elect have a most wonderful learning experience and grow in their personal faith through these workshops, a vast landscape of undiscovered country remains to explore as Presbyterian church officers. Many important topics cannot be addressed in four workshops. New issues arise in the life of the church. Old issues come back to visit. Church officers need to continue their education across their term of service. What are some options for church officer continuing education?

Another book may be needed to adequately deal with this topic, but consider these three suggestions for developing a continuing education component for your church officers.

1. *Questions and Answers.* Previously we mentioned that not all of the questions that arise from readings and discussions in the training sessions can be covered within the time constraints of the workshops. One suggestion was to collect the questions and select one or more to address in a brief (five-minute?) question-and-answer period at the beginning of your session and diaconate meetings. Before providing the official answer, invite the officers to suggest a Presbyterian response. Don't use this as an opportunity to show the officers how much they don't know; instead, encourage their capacity to analyze a question at least to the point of anticipating where to go to find the answer. The pastor(s) or clerk of session or moderator of the board of deacons might handle some questions, but consider assigning the questions to elders or deacons to research and report on during the next Q&A time. Allowing officers to research answers gives them practice and encouragement in finding answers in the constitution or on the denomination's website, or in seeking out people who know the answer.

2. *A Series of Studies.* Use the leadership Bible study passages mentioned in chapters 2 and 4 to explore biblical principles of leadership with the session or diaconate. Use the book *Witness without Parallel: Eight Biblical Texts That Make Us Presbyterian*[1] by Earl S. Johnson to explore the biblical roots of our Presbyterian heritage. Consider a series on a portion of the Study Catechism. An excellent resource for this material is Guy D. Griffith's *Devotion and Discipline: Training for Presbyterian Leaders*,[2] an eight-session guide to the Study Catechism for church leaders, available in both a teacher's and student's guide.

3. *Mini–Case Studies*. Clergy ordained in recent years will remember the case studies that addressed practical issues of Presbyterian polity (e.g., if the parents of a child live out of town and never go to church but the grandparents live locally and are members of your church, can you baptize their grandchild?). Case studies are an engaging way to highlight issues in the church, immediately showing how both the theology and polity of the Presbyterian Church can be applied to practical, real-life situations.

Here is a way to use these mini–case studies in a twenty-five-minute continuing education seminar that can be incorporated into a governing board's stated meetings without lengthening them too much.

• Pick a topic of interest or importance and write a scenario to highlight that topic. Draw situations from your own experience in the church or watch for Presbyterian issues in the denomination or national news.

• Use only one side of a letter-sized page to keep it short.

• Avoid dealing with a topic that is an immediate concern in your congregation at present. Working through theological or polity issues is often easier if they are somewhat removed from the local situation.

• Set the case up so that some sort of decision or response is required by a church officer who is a character in the story.

• Include at the end of the case several standard questions for officers' reflection:

  ◦ How would you respond as an officer to this situation?

  ◦ What is at stake here in terms of theological or polity issues?

  ◦ What specific Presbyterian beliefs or practices address this issue?

  ◦ What specific references in the *Book of Confessions* and/or the *Book of Order* speak to this issue?

• Distribute the printed case study in advance of the meeting for officers to review and consider.

• Take no more than three minutes to welcome everyone, convene the meeting with prayer, and distribute extra copies of the case study as needed.

• Take five minutes or less to review the case, inviting officers to summarize the situation: the setting, the people involved, what happened, and so on. This time will help orient those who may not have studied the case previously.

• Take two minutes to explore some of the ways an officer might respond in that setting.

• Take ten minutes to explore what's at stake, theologically and in terms of polity, in this situation. Why does this matter?

• Invite officers to reveal specific references to the constitution they found helpful. Some officers (may their kind increase) actually find this kind of scavenger hunt through the constitution to be fun, and in the process they develop a working knowledge of the organization and content of these important documents.

• You may want to develop in advance a handout that lists the relevant citations and any other reference material that applies to this situation (Bible passages, position papers, theological statements, etc.).

• Return to the case setting and ask: Having heard what is at stake here and knowing something more about the Presbyterian theology and polity involved, what advice would you give the officer in responding to the situation?

• To close, use a short paragraph, prepared in advance, to summarize both the issue(s) and Presbyterian perspective(s) on the case.

• End with prayer promptly at twenty-five minutes.

Whatever model you use for providing continuing education for your church officers, they, your congregation, and the larger church will benefit from an increasing familiarity with the beliefs and practices that shape who we are and a growing confidence in the application of those beliefs and practices to real life in the church.

Conclusion

The big question for most readers of this book will be: Does this model of church officer training work? In the section that follows, some of the elders and deacons who have gone through the training describe, in their own words, the impact the process had upon them. Their words answer that question far better than I could.

The contributors below represent the three Presbyterian Church (USA) churches that have used this format: First Presbyterian Church, Morganton, North Carolina; Mount Pleasant Presbyterian Church, Mount Pleasant, South Carolina; and Myers Park Presbyterian Church, Charlotte, North Carolina. I have extracted portions of their comments for the sake of brevity, but in all cases the extractions are true to the overall feelings expressed in the full version of what was written.

First Presbyterian Church, Morganton, North Carolina

First Presbyterian Church in Morganton, North Carolina, was the guinea pig! My dissertation for the doctor of ministry degree at Columbia Seminary in Decatur, Georgia, was the impetus for this course. First Church, Morganton used this program from 1993 to 1997. The church had approximately nine hundred members, with an average of three hundred in worship attendance. They have a unicameral system of government with twenty-four elders on the session. Here's what some of them had to say about their training.

* * *

> I have served as an elder for three terms of three years each. The first was in the early '70s and the other two were in the '90s. . . . My second training experience impacted me in a significantly different way. The two parts that readily come to mind were a time of worship each session and sharing faith stories in the chancel of the sanctuary prior to the training sessions. Having a meal together each time was a wonderful way to build community. . . . This spiritual experience was one of the most significant periods of my life.
>
> Anne Wilson, Elder

For me, no training course before or since has compared to this one. It shaped me as an elder and as a person. Worship, faith sharing in the small group, theology, and polity were all integral and vital parts of the whole. . . .

Integrating all four segments—faith sharing, worship, theology, and polity—shaped us as a session and influenced the tone of session meetings. We were not an ecclesiastical board, but a group of disciples doing God's work. God was the center of our meetings.

The training, bonding us as a session as it did, made us feel that we were part of a team—a group of disciples as it were. We became one; we became partners with you. We were all on the same level, having different roles and talents, but equals.

Elsie J. Bartlett, Elder

The small-group experiences were very meaningful for me. I feel there was a special bond established between each of us as we shared our faith stories. Trust relationships were formed. Friendships were made. Mutual respect was established between us. In our small group as we shared our faith stories with each other, there was the common bond of returning to the roots of faith learned in early childhood. . . .

The intensity of the leadership training enhanced and accelerated the growth of the group and led us toward a more unified, productive relationship.

Bridgette Davis, Elder

Being new to the Presbyterian Church, newest and youngest on the session, I felt most appreciative of having such an opportunity. This course gave me the knowledge and confidence necessary to carry out the mission of the church.

Actually, the most memorable things about the course were Communion and both sharing my personal faith story and hearing the faith stories of others. The closeness felt during that time helped me to understand who the fellow session class members were and somewhat mitigated the necessary "business behavior" in the following years of working together in arduous and sometimes stressful situations.

Bob Hensley, Elder

Mount Pleasant Presbyterian Church, Mount Pleasant, South Carolina

Mount Pleasant Presbyterian Church traces its history to 1864. It has recently gone through a tremendous growth phase as the Charleston, South Carolina, area has exploded in population. The church currently has a congregation of twenty-seven hundred members with over twelve hundred in average worship attendance at three services. They have both deacons and elders, with twenty-four in each class. Here's what some of their elders and deacons say about their training.

* * *

I can't remember what I had for lunch, but I can recall a football score twenty-five years ago and that perfect golf shot hit fifteen years ago. I think that was my last perfect shot. Other things I can recall from my "memory banks" are things that affect and change my life, such as the officer training course. The experience greatly impacted my life.

I enjoyed the format of the training. Worship and Communion always set the stage for God's work. It cleanses the heart and mind. The everyday decisions and worries are put aside. This time helped me focus on our task. . . .

We were allowed to look into our "faith journey" and the journey of others. This was a privilege. All Christians have a personal faith with God, but being able to share this experience with others is extraordinary. The small groups were primarily the time we had to do this. I feel this time was too short. . . . This is where we got into the meat of being a Christian and learning about each other.

David Agee, Elder

I was most touched by the love I felt in the room. It was an energy beyond words. We would discuss the material and reflect how that worked into our lives. Sharing was easy and created a bond with those around you. When we broke off into small groups to work on our faith, it went well beyond raising the bar! It was very exhausting, yet cleansing to our soul.

Becoming a deacon was a commitment that I was ready for; however, the love I have received for serving God far exceeded any expectation. I am just learning more about who I am and what purpose God has planned for me.

Pam Miller, Deacon

I would like to say that, having gone through officer training previous to your curriculum, I had never felt as well prepared or had a clear sense of my call to serve prior to experiencing your method of training. Second, the feeling of being part of a team, all having different skill sets or gifts to share, became more evident than it had for me previously. Trying to understand how we each applied our gifts and helping each other through our shortcomings became a part of working as a team.

One thing that you instituted with the group, serving Communion to each other before going into our business meeting, took on a special meaning for me. It put the role of servant in perspective for me and, after all (as you would say), "How can you argue with someone with whom you have just had Communion?" The officers worked as a true "community of faith," and I strongly believe that serving one another played an important part in how we interacted and how we sought to serve God and the congregation of MPPC.

Scott Richardson, Elder

What evidence do I see that this training is effective? Well, the session I serve on today is the first group in which everyone was trained by Steve. We have now gone eleven months since Steve announced his resignation and we have not had an interim pastor, and the church has continued to grow and thrive. (Don't take this personally, Steve, but you trained us so well we've been able to move forward without you.) Initially we all feared what would happen with Steve's leaving, but we realized we were well trained, not just at the beginning but throughout our term as officers, and we'd been empowered to do our ministries and we could continue on to do what we had been trained to do.

Kay Rigter, Elder

Myers Park Presbyterian Church, Charlotte, North Carolina

Myers Park Presbyterian Church in Charlotte, North Carolina, is only seventy-five years old but has been a leader in our denomination for most of those years. The congregation is made up of thirty-eight hundred members who average approximately twelve hundred in worship each week. I became the pastor of the church in August 2002. We've had one class of officers go through this training. Here's what some of them had to say.

* * *

The officer training sessions proved to be a more comprehensive experience than I expected. I felt I was being prepared for a richer, more meaningful relationship with God that will last beyond a specific term on the session. The curriculum knitted together elements of a Christian life that should not be the exclusive purview of only officers. By combining worship, theological study, the heritage of our denomination, and a call to purpose, the sessions became a microcosm of what should be prominent components of our lifelong faith journey. Taking that collective experience and our personal introspection into small groups created a safe haven for open discussion. We could permit ourselves the vulnerability of honesty because a sharing of faith is a sharing of trust. For me, the curriculum built discipleship, and officer training was thereby a natural byproduct.

Mark deCastrique, Elder, Class of 2006

As a new officer at MPPC, I found the training to be invaluable and a way to get to know other officers on a very personal basis. The worship component definitely set a tone of reverence and fellowship, reminding us of our true purpose as disciples, and the study of the *Book of Order* and *Book of Confessions* was extremely enlightening, educating me for the first time on what it really means to be a Presbyterian. The small-group discussions in the combined sessions provided an arena for the officers to get to know one another and share ideas about the church and what we as a community of faith believe to be true. The separate small-group discussions with the same group of officers provided an opportunity for intimacy and sharing that was very rewarding to the members of our group. I never felt like our time together was wasted. . . .

I felt very nurtured throughout the process and believe that all officers would benefit both personally and as a collective body of leaders through participation in this program.

Cheryl Steele, Deacon, Class of 2006

What was wonderful about the experience was that we had time to discuss things in a smaller group setting or even around the dinner table with other disciples. At the same time, we were building relationships with those we will work with on the session. I walked away each night filled with the Spirit and so excited about the thoughts of what we could all do, together, in Jesus's name.

Despite feeling overwhelmed at times, in the end, it was evident that we were building a team of disciples who would each bring their own special gifts and would have to work together. When studying for and taking the oral exam, everything seemed to just come together, and a peace came over me. . . .

I feel so different inside after these experiences. I feel humbled; I feel a specific purpose every time I think of or walk into the church; communion even feels different—so powerful.

> Vicki Garrett, Elder, Class of 2006

I can initially summarize my opinion of the officer training course as excellent, excellent, excellent!!! Having previously been ordained as a deacon in Myers Park Presbyterian Church and later installed at First Presbyterian Church, Columbus, Georgia, this was my first exposure to any course of this type. . . .

The format of having a worship service, with Communion, at the outset really set a good tone for the remainder of each session. It put everyone in a "good feeling," a spiritual mood. None of the three and a half hours was wasted time; all segments were good. But the one I most enjoyed was the small group. It resulted in a "bonding" of our four that will carry over into our service as deacons. . . .

Finally, this training program really brought me up short. It made me realize, in spite of my past experiences as an officer of the church, how weak I was in knowledge of church theology and polity. Certainly we as the deacon class of 2006 are better equipped to serve.

> Ellison Smyth, Deacon, Class of 2006

* * *

An old saying holds that "the proof of the pudding is in the eating," which means that the true value or quality of something can only be judged when put to use. Put more directly, results count. The above excerpts from elders and deacons, based on the results they experienced, would seem to indicate our new model for officer training has something of value to offer the church.

The evaluation form that we use with each class is included in appendix F. Their feedback is most helpful to fine-tune next year's class. Because of their comments, we moved small groups from after worship to the end of the evening, which seems to work better. They helped us split the theology and polity segments with the meal, which also works better than back-to-back segments. The students have also shaped and pruned the lesson plans. Thank God for them!

I have taught some variation of this course over the past ten years. As a result of listening to feedback from all the officers who have gone through the training, I am always changing the process somewhat, hopefully for the better. It's a work-in-progress, as it should be.

Put your DNA on the course and make it yours. Your emphases within theology and polity can make the course distinctively yours. I have also found that each class of officers is unique, and so they change the course as well. The overall structure remains the same, and it works.

Appendix A

STUDY GUIDE FOR NEW ELDERS AND DEACONS

(Many pages in the appendixes are meant to be reproduced for use in the classroom. For ease of use, you may enlarge these pages as desired to fit letter-size paper.)

"[T]he session shall examine them [officers-elect] as to their personal faith; knowledge of the doctrine, government, and discipline contained in the Constitution of the church; and the duties of the office" [G-14.0205].

In addition to your other assignments, these questions will help you prepare for the examination by the session at the end of your training process.

[Note: Most of these questions can be answered by judicious use of the indices in the *Book of Order* and the *Book of Confessions* and your readings in *Called to Serve*.]

1. Personal Faith

1.1   What is the story of how you came to be a person of faith?

1.2   What people have been influential in the development of your faith? In what ways?

1.3   Over the course of your life, what are some of the things that have increased your faith? Which have challenged your faith?

1.4   What are some of the factors that went into your decision to accept the call to be a church officer?

1.5   Which ordination question is the most challenging for you?

1.6   Are there any of the ordination questions that you cannot, in good conscience, answer in the affirmative?

2. Knowledge of Doctrine

2.1   Who is the head of the Presbyterian Church (U.S.A.)?

2.2   What does it mean to say "God alone is Lord of the conscience"?

2.3   Which of the Great Ends of the Church has the highest priority for you?

2.4   What is a confession?

2.5   Why are confessions important in our tradition?

2.6   Why do we have more than one confession?

2.7   How many confessions are in the *Book of Confessions*?

2.8   What is the purpose of the *Book of Confessions*?

2.9   Which two confessions are shared by all Christians worldwide (the Church catholic)?

2.10 Which confessions were formed in the twentieth century, and what were their particular historical contexts?

2.11 What are the watchwords of the Protestant Reformation?

2.12 What is the central affirmation of the Reformed tradition?

2.13 Name one other affirmation of the Reformed tradition.

2.14 What is one element of the mission the church is called to as the body of Christ?

2.15 Why does the Presbyterian Church (U.S.A.) have such a strong emphasis on diversity and inclusiveness?

3. Knowledge of Government

3.1 What documents make up the constitution of the Presbyterian Church (U.S.A.)?

3.2 What are the three parts of the *Book of Order,* and what is each part's special focus?

3.3 Name one of the principles of Presbyterian government.

3.4 What are the three ordained offices in the Presbyterian Church?

3.5 What are the duties and responsibilities of elders and sessions?

3.6 What are the duties and responsibilities of deacons and the board of deacons?

3.7 Name the four governing bodies in the Presbyterian system, and briefly describe their function(s).

3.8 How do you understand this statement from the *Book of Order*: "Presbyters are not simply to reflect the will of the people, but rather to seek together to find and represent the will of Christ"? (G-4.0301d)

4. Knowledge of Worship and Sacraments

4.1 Name the six elements of Christian worship.

4.2 What is the typical order of service (major sections) in Presbyterian worship?

4.3 What part does Scripture play in our worship and life together?

4.4 What is the primary role of music and musicians in worship?

4.5 How many sacraments are celebrated in the Presbyterian Church?

4.6 What are the biblical roots of each of the sacraments?

4.7 What is the significance (meaning) of each of the sacraments?

4.8 What are some of the ways our worship service integrates Scripture, proclamation, prayer, and praise?

5. Knowledge of Discipline

5.1 What is the purpose of church discipline?

5.2 What are the two types of judicial cases?

5.3 What is the difference between a dissent and a protest?

6. Knowledge of the Local Church

(Answers to these questions are specific to a particular congregation.)

6.1 In what year was this church founded? How old is it now?

6.2 How many pastors have served this congregation?

6.3 How many elders and deacons and trustees does this church have?

6.4 Who is the current clerk of session?

6.5 Who is the current moderator of the board of deacons?

6.6 What are the major committees (councils, ministries, work groups, etc.) of the session?

6.7 What are the major committees (or councils, or ministries, etc.) of the diaconate?

6.8 Does this church have a mission statement? If so, what is it?

Study Guide for New Elders and Deacons: Answer Key

"The session shall examine them [officers-elect] as to their personal faith; knowledge of the doctrine, government, and discipline contained in the Constitution of the church; and the duties of the office." [G-14.0205]

In addition to your other assignments, these questions will help you prepare for the examination by the session at the end of your training process.

[Note: Most of these questions can be answered by judicious use of the indices in the *Book of Order* and the *Book of Confessions* and your readings in *Called to Serve*.]

1. Personal Faith

1.1 What is the story of how you came to be a person of faith?

1.2 What people have been influential in the development of your faith? In what ways?

1.3 Over the course of your life, what are some of the things that have challenged and increased your faith?

1.4 What are some of the factors that went into your decision to accept the call to be a church officer?

1.5 Which ordination question is the most challenging for you?

1.6 Are there any of the ordination questions that you cannot, in good conscience, answer in the affirmative?

2 Knowledge of Doctrine

2.1 Who is the head of the Presbyterian Church (U.S.A.)?

G-1.0100a. All power in heaven and earth is given to Jesus Christ by Almighty God, who raised Christ from the dead and set him above all rule and authority, all power and dominion, and every name that is named, not only in this age but also in that which is to come. God has put all things under the Lordship of Jesus Christ and has made Christ Head of the Church, which is his body.

2.2 What does it mean to say "God alone is Lord of the conscience"?

G-1.0301(1)(a) That "God alone is Lord of the conscience, and hath left it free from the doctrines and commandments of men which are in anything contrary to his Word, or beside it, in matters of faith or worship."

G-1.0301(1)(b) Therefore we consider the rights of private judgment, in all matters that respect religion, as universal and unalienable. . . .

2.3 Which of the Great Ends of the Church has the highest priority for you?

G–1.0200 The great ends of the church are the proclamation of the gospel for the salvation of humankind; the shelter, nurture, and spiritual fellowship of the children of God; the maintenance of divine worship; the preservation of the truth; the promotion of social righteousness; and the exhibition of the Kingdom of Heaven to the world.

2.4 What is a confession?

A statement of what we believe; an expression of the doctrines of the faith.

2.5 Why are confessions important in our tradition?

G-2.0100b. These statements identify the church as a community of people known by its convictions as well as by its actions. They guide the church in its study and interpretation of the Scriptures; they summarize the essence of Christian tradition; they direct the church in maintaining sound doctrines; they equip the church for its work of proclamation.

2.6 Why do we have more than one confession?

[Because the Church acknowledges the dynamic nature of belief arising out of particular circumstances and contexts. We cannot, in any one moment of time, express a statement of faith for all of time.]

G-2.0500b. Thus, the creeds and confessions of this church reflect a particular stance within the history of God's people. They are the result of prayer, thought, and experience within a living tradition.

2.7 How many confessions are in the *Book of Confessions*?

There are eleven.

2.8 What is the purpose of the *Book of Confessions*?

G-2.0100a. The Presbyterian Church (U.S.A.) states its faith and bears witness to God's grace in Jesus Christ in the creeds and confessions in *The Book of Confessions*. In these confessional statements the church declares to its members and to the world who and what it is, what it believes, what it resolves to do.

G–2.0500b. . . . They serve to strengthen personal commitment and the life and witness of the community of believers.

2.9 Which two confessions are shared by all Christians worldwide (the Church catholic)?

The Apostles' Creed and the Nicene Creed

2.10 Which confessions were formed in the twentieth century, and what were their particular historical contexts?

The Theological Declaration of Barmen (1934)—the rise of Nazi Germany—focus on the Lordship of Jesus Christ.

The Confession of 1967—the civil rights movement—focus on reconciliation.

The Brief Statement of Faith (1983)—the reunion of the northern and southern Presbyterian churches.

2.11 What are the watchwords of the Protestant Reformation?

G-2.0400 Faith of the Protestant Reformation

In its confessions, the Presbyterian Church (U.S.A.) identifies with the affirmations of the Protestant Reformation. The focus of these affirmations is the rediscovery of God's grace in Jesus Christ as revealed in the Scriptures. The Protestant watchwords—grace alone, faith alone, Scripture alone—embody principles of understanding which continue to guide and motivate the people of God in the life of faith.

2.12 What is the central affirmation of the Reformed tradition?

G-2.0500a. In its confessions, the Presbyterian Church (U.S.A.) expresses the faith of the Reformed tradition. Central to this tradition is the affirmation of the majesty, holiness, and providence of God who creates, sustains, rules, and redeems the world in the freedom of sovereign righteousness and love.

2.13 Name one other affirmation of the Reformed tradition.

. . . Related to this central affirmation of God's sovereignty are other great themes of the Reformed tradition:

G-2.0500a.(1) The election of the people of God for service as well as for salvation;

(2) Covenant life marked by a disciplined concern for order in the church according to the Word of God;

(3) A faithful stewardship that shuns ostentation and seeks proper use of the gifts of God's creation;

(4) The recognition of the human tendency to idolatry and tyranny, which calls the people of God to work for the transformation of society by seeking justice and living in obedience to the Word of God.

2.14 What is one element of the mission the church is called to as the body of Christ?

G-3.0200a. The Church is called to be *a sign in and for the world of the new reality* which God has made available to people in Jesus Christ.

G-3.0200c. The Church is *the body of Christ*, both in its corporate life and in the lives of its individual members, and is called *to give shape and substance to this truth*.

G-3.0300a. The Church is called to tell the good news of salvation by the grace of God through faith in Jesus Christ as the only Savior and Lord, proclaiming in Word and Sacrament that . . . (see G-3.0300a[1, 2])

G-3.0300b. The Church is called to present the claims of Jesus Christ, leading persons to repentance, acceptance of him as Savior and Lord, and new life as his disciples.

G-3.0300c. The Church is called to be Christ's faithful evangelist . . . (see G-3.0300c[1–3]).

G-3.0400 Called to Risk and Trust—The Church is called to undertake this mission even at the risk of losing its life, trusting in God alone as the author and giver of life, sharing the gospel, and doing those deeds in the world that point beyond themselves to the new reality in Christ.

G-3.0401 Called to Openness—The Church is called

a. to a new openness to the presence of God in the Church and in the world, to more fundamental obedience, and to a more joyous celebration in worship and work;

b. to a new openness to its own membership, by affirming itself as a community of diversity, becoming in fact as well as in faith a community of women and men of all ages, races, and conditions, and by providing for inclusiveness as a visible sign of the new humanity;

c. to a new openness to the possibilities and perils of its institutional forms in order to ensure the faithfulness and usefulness of these forms to God's activity in the world;

d. to a new openness to God's continuing reformation of the Church ecumenical, that it might be a more effective instrument of mission in the world.

2.15 Why does the Presbyterian Church (U.S.A.) have such a strong emphasis on diversity and inclusiveness?

G-4.0401 Variety of Forms—The church in its witness to the uniqueness of the Christian faith is called to mission and must be responsive to diversity in both the church and the world. Thus the fellowship of Christians as it gathers for worship and orders its corporate life will display a rich variety of form, practice, language, program, nurture, and service to suit culture and need.

G-4.0402 Openness to Others—Our unity in Christ enables and requires the church to be open to all persons and to the varieties of talents and gifts of God's people, including those who are in the communities of the arts and sciences.

3. Knowledge of Government

3.1   What documents make up the constitution of the Presbyterian Church (U.S.A.)?

G-1.0500 5. The Constitution Defined—The *Constitution of the Presbyterian Church (U.S.A.)* consists of the *Book of Confessions* and the *Book of Order*.

3.2   What are the three parts of the *Book of Order,* and what is each part's special focus?

G-1.0502 The *Book of Order* includes:

Form of Government[—how we are organized to do our work]

Directory for Worship[—how we, both corporately and privately, offer our lives in worship]

Rules of Discipline[—how we are to deal with times of dissention and conflict].

3.3   Name one of the principles of Presbyterian government.

G-4.0301a. The particular churches of the Presbyterian Church (U.S.A.) wherever they are, taken collectively, constitute one church;

b. This church shall be governed by presbyters (elders and ministers of the Word and Sacrament, traditionally called ruling and teaching elders);

c. These presbyters shall come together in governing bodies (traditionally called judicatories or courts) in regular gradation;

d. Presbyters are not simply to reflect the will of the people, but rather to seek together to find and represent the will of Christ;

e. Decisions shall be reached in governing bodies by vote, following opportunity for discussion, and a majority shall govern;

f. A higher governing body shall have the right of review and control over a lower one and shall have power to determine matters of controversy upon reference, complaint, or appeal;

g. Presbyters are ordained only by the authority of a governing body;

h. Ecclesiastical jurisdiction is a shared power, to be exercised jointly by presbyters gathered in governing bodies;

i. Governing bodies possess whatever administrative authority is necessary to give effect to duties and powers assigned by the Constitution of the church.

3.4   What are the three ordained offices in the Presbyterian Church?

G-6.0103 Offices Named—The Church offices mentioned in the New Testament which this church has maintained include those of presbyters (ministers of the Word and Sacrament and elders) and deacons.

3.5 What are the duties and responsibilities of elders and sessions?

G-6.0304 Specific Responsibilities—It is the duty of elders, individually and jointly, to strengthen and nurture the faith and life of the congregation committed to their charge. Together with the pastor, they should encourage the people in the worship and service of God, equip and renew them for their tasks within the church and for their mission in the world, visit and comfort and care for the people, with special attention to the poor, the sick, the lonely, and those who are oppressed. They should inform the pastor and session of those persons and structures which may need special attention. They should assist in worship. (See W-1.4003, W-2.3011–.3012, W-3.1003, W-3.3616, and W-4.4003.) They should cultivate their ability to teach the Bible and may be authorized to supply places which are without the regular ministry of the Word and Sacrament. In specific circumstances and with proper instruction, specific elders may be authorized by the presbytery to administer the Lord's Supper in accord with G-11.0103z. Those duties which all Christians are bound to perform by the law of love are especially incumbent upon elders because of their calling to office and are to be fulfilled by them as official responsibilities.

See also G-10.0102 (a–s) for a list of nineteen detailed responsibilities.

3.6 What are the duties and responsibilities of deacons and the board of deacons?

G-6.0402 Responsibilities—It is the duty of deacons, first of all, to minister to those who are in need, to the sick, to the friendless, and to any who may be in distress both within and beyond the community of faith. They shall assume such other duties as may be delegated to them from time to time by the session, such as leading the people in worship through prayers of intercession, reading the Scriptures, presenting the gifts of the people, and assisting with the Lord's Supper. (See W-3.3416.)

3.7 Name the four governing bodies in the Presbyterian system, and briefly describe their function(s).

G-9.0101 Definition—The Presbyterian Church (U.S.A.) shall be governed by representative bodies composed of presbyters, both elders and ministers of the Word and Sacrament. These governing bodies shall be called

session [which governs the particular, local congregation]

presbytery [which governs a regional group of congregations]

synod [which governs a group of presbyteries]

General Assembly [which governs all presbyteries as a denomination].

3.8 How do you understand this statement from the *Book of Order*:

"Presbyters are not simply to reflect the will of the people, but rather to seek together to find and represent the will of Christ"?

Commissioners to governing bodies are not sent with instructions from their constituency, but are expected to seek to discern God's will together in the midst of the governing body's deliberations. No governing body can "bind the conscience" of its commissioner—that is, compel them to vote in a certain way.

4. Knowledge of Worship and Sacraments

4.1 Name the six elements of Christian worship.

W-2.1000 Prayer

W-2.2000 Scripture Read and Proclaimed

W-2.3000 Baptism

W-2.4000 The Lord's Supper

W-2.5000 Self-Offering

W-2.6000 Relating to Each Other and the World

4.2 What is the typical order of service (major sections) in Presbyterian worship?

W–3.3202:

(1) gathering around the Word;

(2) proclaiming the Word;

(3) responding to the Word;

(4) the sealing of the Word;

(5) bearing and following the Word into the world.

4.3 What part does Scripture play in our worship and life together?

W-2.2001 Centrality of Scripture—The church confesses the Scriptures to be the Word of God written, witnessing to God's self-revelation. Where that Word is read and proclaimed, Jesus Christ the Living Word is present by the inward witness of the Holy Spirit. For this reason the reading, hearing, preaching, and confessing of the Word are central to Christian worship. The session shall ensure that in public worship the Scripture is read and proclaimed regularly in the common language(s) of the particular church.

4.4 What is the primary role of music and musicians in worship?

W-2.1004 Music as Prayer: Choir and Instrumental Music—To lead the congregation in the singing of prayer is a primary role of the choir and other musicians. They also may pray on behalf of the congregation with introits, responses, and other musical forms. Instrumental music may be a form of prayer since words are not essential to prayer. In worship, music is not to be for entertainment or artistic display. Care should be taken that it not be used merely as a cover for silence. Music as prayer is to be a worthy offering to God on behalf of the people. (See also W-2.2008; W-3.3101)

4.5   How many sacraments are celebrated in the Presbyterian Church?

Only two.

W-1.3033(2) The Reformed tradition understands Baptism and the Lord's Supper to be Sacraments, instituted by God and commended by Christ.

4.6   What are the biblical roots of each of the sacraments?

See annotations for W-2.3000 and 2.4000 in the *Book of Order* for specific scriptural references.

W-2.3001 Jesus and Baptism—Baptism is the sign and seal of incorporation into Christ. Jesus through his own baptism identified himself with sinners in order to fulfill all righteousness. Jesus in his own baptism was attested Son by the Father and was anointed with the Holy Spirit to undertake the way of the servant manifested in his sufferings, death, and resurrection. Jesus the risen Lord assured his followers of his continuing presence and power and commissioned them "Go therefore and make disciples of all nations, baptizing them in the name of the Father and of the Son and of the Holy Spirit, and teaching them to obey everything that I have commanded you. And remember, I am with you always, to the end of the age" (Matt. 28:19, NRSV).

W-2.4001 Jesus and the Supper

Jesus Shared Meals

W-2.4001a. The Lord's Supper is the sign and seal of eating and drinking in communion with the crucified and risen Lord. During his earthly ministry Jesus shared meals with his followers as a sign of community and acceptance and as an occasion for his own ministry. He celebrated Israel's feasts of covenant commemoration.

Last Supper

W-2.4001b. In his last meal before his death Jesus took and shared with his disciples the bread and wine, speaking of them as his body and blood, signs of the new covenant. He commended breaking bread and sharing a cup to remember and proclaim his death.

Resurrection

W-2.4001c. On the day of his resurrection, the risen Jesus made himself known to his followers in the breaking of bread. He continued to show himself to believers, by blessing and breaking bread, by preparing, serving, and sharing common meals. (W-1.3033)

4.7 What is the significance (meaning) of each of the sacraments?

Baptism

W-2.3001 Jesus and Baptism—Baptism is the sign and seal of incorporation into Christ. . . .

W-2.3002 Dying and Rising in Baptism—In Baptism, we participate in Jesus' death and resurrection. In Baptism, we die to what separates us from God and are raised to newness of life in Christ. Baptism points us back to the grace of God expressed in Jesus Christ, who died for us and who was raised for us. Baptism points us forward to that same Christ who will fulfill God's purpose in God's promised future.

The Lord's Supper

W-2.4001a. The Lord's Supper is the sign and seal of eating and drinking in communion with the crucified and risen Lord. . . .

W-2.4004 Remembering—At the Lord's Table, the Church is

a. renewed and empowered by the memory of Christ's life, death, resurrection, and promise to return;

b. sustained by Christ's pledge of undying love and continuing presence with God's people;

c. sealed in God's covenant of grace through partaking of Christ's self-offering.

In remembering, believers receive and trust the love of Christ present to them and to the world; they manifest the reality of the covenant of grace in reconciling and being reconciled; and they proclaim the power of Christ's reign for the renewal of the world in justice and in peace.

W-2.4006 Communion of the Faithful— . . . Each time they gather at the Table the believing community

a. are united with the Church in every place, and the whole Church is present;

b. join with all the faithful in heaven and on earth in offering thanksgiving to the triune God;

c. renew the vows taken at Baptism;

and they commit themselves afresh to love and serve God, one another, and their neighbors in the world.

4.8 What are some of the ways our worship service integrates Scripture, proclamation, prayer, and praise?

Specific to each local congregation's practice and setting.

5. Knowledge of Discipline

5.1 What is the purpose of church discipline?

D-1.0101 Church Discipline—Church discipline is the church's exercise of authority given by Christ, both in the direction of guidance, control, and nurture of its members and in the direction of constructive criticism of offenders. Thus, the purpose of discipline is to honor God by making clear the significance of membership in the body of Christ; to preserve the purity of the church by nourishing the individual within the life of the believing community; to correct or restrain wrongdoing in order to bring members to repentance and restoration; to restore the unity of the church by removing the causes of discord and division; and to secure the just, speedy, and economical determination of proceedings. In all respects, members are to be accorded procedural safeguards and due process, and it is the intention of these rules so to provide.

5.2 What are the two types of judicial cases?

D-2.0201 Remedial or Disciplinary—Judicial process consists of two types of cases: remedial and disciplinary.

D-2.0202 Remedial—A remedial case is one in which an irregularity or a delinquency of a lower governing body, the General Assembly Council, or an entity of the General Assembly may be corrected by a higher governing body.

D-2.0203 Disciplinary—A disciplinary case is one in which a church member or officer may be censured for an offense.

5.3 What is the difference between a dissent and a protest?

G-9.0303 Dissent—A dissent is a declaration expressing disagreement with the action or decision of a governing body. A dissent shall be made at the particular session of the governing body during which the action or decision dissented from is taken. The name or names of the members dissenting shall be recorded.

G-9.0304 Protest—A protest is a written declaration, supported by reasons, expressing disagreement with what is believed by one or more members of a governing body to be an irregularity or a delinquency.

6. Knowledge of the Local Church

(Answers to these questions are specific to a particular congregation.)

6.1 In what year was this church founded?

6.2   How many pastors have served this congregation?

6.3   How many elders and deacons and trustees does this church have?

6.4   Who is the current clerk of session?

6.5   Who is the current moderator of the board of deacons?

6.6   What are the major committees (councils, ministries, work groups, etc.) of the session?

6.7   What are the major committees (or councils, or ministries, etc.) of the diaconate?

6.8   Does this church have a mission statement? If so, what is it?

BOOK OF CONFESSIONS PRESENTATION OUTLINE

Adapted from material in the prefaces to *The Book of Confessions* and the preface to each individual confession.

The Book of Confessions

Part 1 of the Constitution of the Presbyterian Church (U.S.A.)

To Confess

To confess means openly to affirm, declare, acknowledge, or take a stand for what one believes to be true.

The truth that is confessed may include the admission of sin and guilt but is more than that.

When Christians make a confession, they say,

"This is what we most assuredly believe, regardless of what others may believe and regardless of the opposition, rejection, or persecution that may come to us for taking this stand."

What a Confession Is . . .

An act of Christian faith

All Christians are by definition people who confess their faith—people who make their own the earliest Christian confession: "Jesus Christ is Lord."

A document of Christian faith

An officially adopted statement that spells out a church's understanding of the meaning and implications of the one basic confession of the lordship of Christ.

The Three Directions of Confessions of Faith

God

Confessions of faith are first of all the church's solemn and thankful response to God's self-revelation, expressed with a sense of responsibility to be faithful and obedient to God.

The church itself

Members of a Christian community seek to make clear to themselves who they are, what they believe, and what they resolve to do.

The world

Christians confess their common faith not only to praise and serve God and not only to establish their self-identity but to speak to the world a unified word that declares who they are and what they stand for and against.

The Time for Confession

Throughout the history of the Christian movement, churches have written confessions of faith because they feel that they must do so, not just because they think it would be a good idea.

Confessions of faith may result from a sense of urgent need to correct some distortion of the truth and claim of the gospel that threatens the integrity of the church's faith and life from within the church.

They may result from some political or cultural movement outside the church that openly attacks or subtly seeks to compromise its commitment to the gospel.

Sometimes the urgency to confess comes from the church's conviction that it has a great new insight into the promises and demands of the gospel that is desperately needed by both church and world.

Confessions are written when the church faces a situation of life or a situation of death so urgent that it cannot remain silent but must speak, even at the cost of its own security, popularity, and success.

The Content of Confessions of Faith

At the heart of all confessions is the earliest confession of the New Testament church, "Jesus is Lord."

Sometimes the situation required a short pointed confession dealing with one or more specific issues.

Sometimes, confessions are short summaries of elements of the whole of Christian faith.

The Functions of Confessions

Worship

Defense of orthodoxy

Instruction

Rallying point in times of danger and persecution

Church order and discipline

The Historical Limitations of Confessions

Confessions address the issues, problems, dangers, and opportunities of a given historical situation.

Confessions have been deliberately or unconsciously expressed in the language and thought forms that were commonly accepted when they were written.

Confessions have also distorted the truth revealed in Jesus Christ, been unable to grasp parts of the biblical witness to God's presence and work in Christ, and divided the church into churches with conflicting views of what Christian faith and life are all about.

Reformed Confessions Emphasize

The ecumenical character of Reformed churches

Faith *and* practice—belief *and* action

The claim of God on *all* life

Grace *and* law

Authority of Confessions in the Reformed Tradition

The multiplicity of confessions, written by many people in many places over such a great span of time, means that the Reformed tradition has never been content to recognize any *one* confession or *collection* of confessions as an absolute, infallible statement of the faith of Reformed Christians for all time.

Confessional Authority Is . . .

Provisional authority

All confessions are the work of limited, fallible, sinful human beings and churches.

Temporary authority

Faith in the living God present and at work in the risen Christ through the Holy Spirit means always being open to hear a new and fresh word from the Lord.

Relative authority

They are subordinate to the higher authority of Scripture, which is the norm for discerning the will and work of God in every time and place.

Overview of *The Book of Confessions*

The Book of Confessions

Eleven historical statements reflecting

Date(s)

Location

Historical context/issues/themes

(Information on these three areas is given in the chart below.)

Confessions Catholic (universal)

Nicene Creed

325	Nicaea	Constantine, Roman emperor, converted to Christianity, sought to address disputes

| 381 | Constantinople | Nature of Christ—was the divinity of Christ *created* by God or the *same as* God? |

Apostles' Creed

180	Rome	Marcionite heresy: Jesus was not OT Messiah
2nd/3rd c.	N. Africa	Forgiveness of sins
4th/5th c.	Gaul	Holy, catholic church
5th c.	Rome	He descended into hell
8th c.		(finalized as we know it)

Scots Confession

| 1560 | Scotland | Scottish Parliament declares Scotland a Protestant nation; commissioned new confession of faith; John Knox; emphasizes God's providence and calls for trust and commitment in turbulent times |

Heidelberg Catechism

| 1562–63 | Germany | Tension between Reformed and Lutheran movements: nature of Christ's presence in Lord's Supper; creed states what both can affirm; based on Romans 7:24–25 |

Confessions of the Reformation Era
(Sixteenth- to Eighteenth-Century Confessions)

Second Helvetic Confession

| 1561 | Switzerland | Swiss-German Reformed Church—Bullinger wrote it as part of his Last Will and Testament; used by Frederick (Governor) as defense; adopted by churches of Switzerland |

Westminster Confession

1647	England	English government called for settling issues of Church governance and liturgy; Westminster Assembly convened; political and religious conflicts; civil war; adopted later by other countries
1647	Scotland	
1729	America	
1903	(addendum)	

Shorter Catechism

| 1649 | England | Westminster Assembly (above) |

Larger Catechism

| 1649 | England | Westminster Assembly (above) |

Confessions of the Modern Era

(Twentieth-Century Confessions)

Theological Declaration of Barmen

| 1934 | Germany | Rise of Nazi Germany, WWII; equating nationalism, militarism, and patriotism (under Hitler) with Christianity; there is only one Lord, Jesus Christ, who is Lord over every area of life |

Confession of 1967

| 1967 | USA | UPC(USA); turbulent 1960s; concurrent with Vatican II; prompted by request to revise the Westminster Confession; themes of reconciliation and the Church's role in the world; addressed need to interpret Scripture; *Book of Confessions* adopted |

A Brief Statement of Faith

| 1983 | USA | Reunion of northern and southern branches of Presbyterianism in USA to form PC(USA); articulates common identity in midst of diversity and disagreement; gender inclusiveness, care for God's creation; "In life and in death, we belong to God" |

A New Confession?

Confessional Documents Process

a. Amendments to the confessional documents of this church may be made only in the following manner:

(1) The approval of the proposed amendment by the **General Assembly** and its recommendation to the presbyteries;

(2) The approval in writing of **two thirds of the presbyteries**;

(3) The approval and enactment by the next ensuing **General Assembly**.

b. Before such amendments to the confessional documents shall be transmitted to the presbyteries, the General Assembly shall appoint a **committee of elders and ministers**, numbering not less than fifteen, to consider the proposal, of whom not more than two shall be from any one synod. This committee shall consult with the committee or governing body (or in the latter case an agent thereof) in which the amendment originated, and report its recommendation to the next ensuing General Assembly.

Theology Matters

What we believe shapes our actions and our perspectives.

It is not an option to believe in nothing. The only question is, in *what* and in *whom* do we believe?

For Presbyterians, we believe in Jesus Christ to which the Holy Scriptures and our *Book of Confessions* bear witness.

Appendix C

WORSHIP SERVICES FOR THE FOUR TRAINING SESSIONS

Session I

Call to Worship

Leader: The Lord be with you.

People: And also with you.

Prayer of Confession

Leader: Lord, I have sinned against you,

    in thought (silence)

      in word (silence)

        in deed (silence).

All: Hear my prayer and forgive my sin. Renew within me a right spirit, O God. Through Christ we pray. Amen.

Assurance of Pardon

Leader: In the name of Christ, we are forgiven.

People: Thanks be to God! Amen.

Scripture Reading

Numbers 11:10–17

> Moses heard the people weeping throughout their families, all at the entrances of their tents. Then the LORD became very angry, and Moses was displeased. So Moses said to the LORD, "Why have you treated your servant so badly? Why have I not found favor in your sight, that you lay the burden of all this people on me? Did I conceive all this people? Did I give birth to them, that you should say to me, 'Carry them in your bosom, as a nurse carries a sucking child,' to the land that you promised on oath to their ancestors? Where am I to get meat to give all this people? For they come weeping to me and say, 'Give us meat to eat!' I am not able to carry all this people alone, for they are too heavy for me. If this is the way you are going to treat me, put me to death at once—if I have found favor in your sight—and do not let me see my misery." So the LORD said to Moses, "Gather for me seventy of the elders of Israel, whom you know to be the elders of the people and officers over them; bring them to the tent of meeting, and have them take their place there with you. I will come down and talk with you there; and I will take some of the spirit that is on you and put it on them; and they shall bear the burden of the people along with you so that you will not bear it all by yourself."

Meditation on the Text

Prayers

Communion

Benediction

Session II

Call to Worship

Leader: The Lord be with you.

People: And also with you.

Hymn #513—Let Us Break Bread Together

Prayer of Confession

Leader: God has chosen you to be a leader in the Church:

"Elders should be persons of faith, dedication, and good judgment. Their manner of life should be a demonstration of the Christian gospel, both within the church and in the world." (*BoO* G-6.0303)[1]

"[Deacons should be p]ersons of spiritual character, honest repute, of exemplary lives, brotherly and sisterly love, warm sympathies, and sound judgment. . . ." (*BoO* G-6.0401)[2]

Where is your weakness in being this person? In silence, confess your sin to God and ask God to strengthen you for service. (Silence.)

Assurance of Pardon

Leader: Have you not known? Have you not heard? The LORD is the ever-lasting God, the Creator of the ends of the earth. He does not faint or grow weary; his understanding is unsearchable. He gives power to the faint, and strengthens the powerless. (Isa. 40:28–29)

People: In the name of Jesus Christ, our sins are forgiven!

All: Thanks be to God! Amen.

Scripture Reading

Mark 6:30–44

Narrator: The apostles gathered around Jesus, and told him all that they had done and taught. He said to them,

Jesus: "Come away to a deserted place all by yourselves and rest a while."

Narrator: For many were coming and going, and they had no leisure even to eat. And they went away in the boat to a deserted place by themselves. Now many saw them going and recognized them, and they hurried there on foot from all the towns and arrived ahead of them. As he went ashore, he saw a great crowd; and he had compassion for them, because they were like sheep without a shepherd; and he began to teach them many things. When it grew late, his disciples came to him and said,

Disciples: "This is a deserted place, and the hour is now very late; send them away so that they may go into the surrounding country and villages and buy something for themselves to eat."

Narrator: But he answered them,

Jesus: "You give them something to eat."

Narrator: They said to him,

Disciples: "Are we to go and buy two hundred denarii worth of bread, and give it to them to eat?"

Narrator: And he said to them,

Jesus: "How many loaves have you? Go and see."

Narrator: When they had found out, they said,

Disciples: "Five, and two fish."

Narrator: Then he ordered them to get all the people to sit down in groups on the green grass. So they sat down in groups of hundreds and of fifties. Taking the five loaves and the two fish, he looked up to heaven, and blessed and broke the loaves, and gave them to his disciples to set before the people; and he divided the two fish among them all. And all ate and were filled; and they took up twelve baskets full of broken pieces of the fish. Those who had eaten the loaves numbered five thousand men.

Reflection on Scripture

Prayers of the People

(Each bidding prayer followed by "Lord, hear our prayer" in unison.)

The Lord's Prayer

Communion

Benediction

Notes

1. Presbyterian Church (U.S.A.), *Book of Order 2003/2004* (Louisville, Ky.: Published by the Office of the General Assembly).

2. Ibid.

Session III

Call to Worship

Leader: The Lord be with you.

People: And also with you.

Hymn: #316—Breathe on Me, Breath of God

Prayer of Confession

Leader: Lord, if I were to completely sell out to being your faithful disciple, what would have to change in my life? (Silence.)

Assurance of Pardon

Leader: Hear the Good News!

People: In Jesus Christ our sins are forgiven!

Doxology

Scripture Reading (unison)

Acts 1:8; 2:1–4, 43–47

"But you will receive power when the Holy Spirit has come upon you; and you will be my witnesses in Jerusalem, in all Judea and Samaria, and to the ends of the earth.". . .

When the day of Pentecost had come, they were all together in one place. And suddenly from heaven there came a sound like the rush of a violent wind, and it filled the entire house where they were sitting. Divided tongues, as of fire, appeared among them, and a tongue rested on each of them. All of them were filled with the Holy Spirit and began to speak in other languages, as the Spirit gave them ability. . . .

Awe came upon everyone, because many wonders and signs were being done by the apostles. All who believed were together and had all things in common; they would sell their possessions and goods and distribute the proceeds to all, as any had need. Day by day, as they spent much time together in the temple, they broke bread at home and ate their food with glad and generous hearts, praising God and having the goodwill of all the people. And day by day the Lord added to their number those who were being saved.

Reflection on Scripture

Prayers of the People

(Each bidding prayer followed by "Lord, hear our prayer" in unison.)

The Lord's Prayer

Communion

Benediction

Session IV

Call to Worship

Leader: The Lord be with you.

People: And also with you.

Hymn: #126—Come, Holy Spirit, Heavenly Dove

Litany of Penitence

Leader: Let us pray.

All: Holy and merciful God,
we confess to you and to one another,
and to the whole communion of saints in heaven and on earth,
that we have sinned by our own fault
in thought, word, and deed,
by what we have done,
and by what we have left undone.
Leader: We have not loved you with our whole heart, and mind, and strength.
We have not loved our neighbors as ourselves.
We have not forgiven others as we have been forgiven.
People: Have mercy on us, O God.
Leader: We have not listened to your call to serve as Christ served us.
We have not been true to the mind of Christ.
We have grieved your Holy Spirit.
People: Have mercy on us, O God.
Leader: We confess to you, O God, all our past unfaithfulness:
the pride, hypocrisy, and impatience in our lives,
People: we confess to you, O God.
Leader: Our self-indulgent appetites and ways
and our exploitation of other people,
People: we confess to you, O God.
Leader: Our anger at our own frustration
and our envy of those more fortunate than ourselves,
People: we confess to you, O God.
Leader: Our intemperate love of worldly goods and comforts,
and our dishonesty in daily life and work,
People: we confess to you, O God.
Leader: Our negligence in prayer and worship,
and our failure to commend the faith that is in us,
People: we confess to you, O God.
Leader: Accept our repentance, O God,
for the wrongs we have done.

for our neglect of human need and suffering
and our indifference to injustice and cruelty,
People: accept our repentance, O God.
Leader: For all false judgments,
for uncharitable thoughts toward our neighbors,
and for our prejudice and contempt
toward those who differ from us,
People: accept our repentance, O God.
Leader: For our waste and pollution of your creation
and our lack of concern for those who come after us,
People: accept our repentance, O God.
Leader: Restore us, O God,
and let your anger depart from us.
People: Favorably hear us, O God,
for your mercy is great. Amen.   *Book of Common Worship*[1]

Assurance of Pardon

> Leader: Hear the Good News!
>
> **People: In Jesus Christ our sins are forgiven!**

Scripture Reading (unison)

Ephesians 4:11–16

> The gifts he gave were that some would be apostles, some prophets, some evangelists, some pastors and teachers, to equip the saints for the work of ministry, for building up the body of Christ, until all of us come to the unity of the faith and of the knowledge of the Son of God, to maturity, to the measure of the full stature of Christ. We must no longer be children, tossed to and fro and blown about by every wind of doctrine, by people's trickery, by their craftiness in deceitful scheming. But speaking the truth in love, we must grow up in every way into him who is the head, into Christ, from whom the whole body, joined and knit together by every ligament with which it is equipped, as each part is working properly, promotes the body's growth in building itself up in love.

Reflection on the Scripture

Prayers of the People

> (Each bidding prayer followed by "Lord, hear our prayer" in unison.)

The Lord's Prayer

Communion

Hymn: #513—Let Us Break Bread Together

> (To be sung during Communion)

Benediction

Notes

1. *Book of Common Worship* (Louisville, Ky.: Westminster/John Knox Press, 1993).

Appendix D

THEOLOGY AND POLITY WORKSHEETS AND HANDOUTS

Worksheet 2

Jesus Christ is Lord

Romans 10:5–17

Read the passage below. The key verse is in bold typeface.

5 Moses writes concerning the righteousness that comes from the law, that "the person who does these things will live by them." [6]But the righteousness that comes from faith says, "Do not say in your heart, 'Who will ascend into heaven?'" (that is, to bring Christ down) [7]"or 'Who will descend into the abyss?'" (that is, to bring Christ up from the dead). [8]But what does it say?

"The word is near you,

on your lips and in your heart"

(that is, the word of faith that we proclaim); [9]**because if you confess with your lips that Jesus is Lord and believe in your heart that God raised him from the dead, you will be saved.** [10]For one believes with the heart and so is justified, and one confesses with the mouth and so is saved. [11]The scripture says, "No one who believes in him will be put to shame." [12]For there is no distinction between Jew and Greek; the same Lord is Lord of all and is generous to all who call on him. [13]For, "Everyone who calls on the name of the Lord shall be saved."

14 But how are they to call on one in whom they have not believed? And how are they to believe in one of whom they have never heard? And how are they to hear without someone to proclaim him? [15]And how are they to proclaim him unless they are sent? As it is written, "How beautiful are the feet of those who bring good news!" [16]But not all have obeyed the good news; for Isaiah says, "Lord, who has believed our message?" [17]So faith comes from what is heard, and what is heard comes through the word of Christ.

Questions for Reflection

1. What do Christians mean when they say that Jesus Christ is "my Lord and Savior"?

2. In your opinion, is Christianity the only true religion?

3. In your opinion, will all human beings be saved?

4. In your opinion, how will God deal with the followers of other religions?

Worksheet 3

PRINCIPLES OF PRESBYTERIAN POLITY

From your readings, fill in the blanks:	if found in *Book of Order* . . . if found in *Called to Serve* . . .	Cite Reference (e.g., G-1.0200) Cite page #
THE HEAD OF THE CHURCH		
1. _____ _____ is the head of the Church.		
THE GREAT ENDS OF THE CHURCH		
2. The Church exists for the _____ of humankind.		
3. The Church exists for the _____, _____, and the _____ _____of the children of God.		
4. The Church exists for the _____ of divine _____.		
5. The Church exists for the preservation of _____.		
6. The Church exists for the promotion of _____ _____.		
7. The Church exists for the exhibition of the _____ of _____ to the world.		
HISTORICAL PRINCIPLES OF CHURCH ORDER		
8. _____ _____ is Lord of the conscience; this means that _____ of _____ is a fundamental right along with the _____ of church and _____.		
9. Every church has the right to establish the _____ of _____ into its fellowship and the _____ of its ministers and members.		
10. Jesus Christ appointed officers, not only to preach and administer the sacraments, but also to _____ _____.		
11. _____ is in order to goodness.		
12. People of good conscience can have _____ _____ . . . and need to exercise _____ _____ toward each other.		
13. The right to elect members of a society rests in _____ _____.		
14. The _____ _____ are the only rule of faith and conduct.		
HISTORICAL PRINCIPLES OF CHURCH GOVERNMENT		
15. The several different congregations constitute _____ _____ of Christ.		
16. A _____ part of the church . . . shall govern the _____.		
17. A _____ shall govern.		
18. Appeals should be made from _____ to _____ governing bodies and that final decisions should be made by the _____ _____ and _____ _____ of the whole Church.		

THE PRESBYTERIAN/REFORMED TRADITION

Reformed Tradition in Historical Context

- Children of God
- Children of Abraham (the Jews)
- Christians
- Roman Catholic Christians
- Protestant Christian
- Reformed Christians
- Presbyterians PC(USA)

The Protestant Reformation

- Reforming the Roman Catholic Church
- Martin Luther challenged the abuses of the church system
  - Indulgences—salvation by works
  - Scriptures interpreted only by clergy
- Church authority vs. Scriptural
- Return to Grace alone, Faith alone, Scripture alone

The Reformed Reformation

- Developed by Swiss reformers in the sixteenth century
  - Ulrich Zwingli
  - John Calvin (Frenchman who made his home in Geneva)
- Became alternative to Lutherans and Anabaptists

Major Beliefs of the Catholic Tradition

- One holy, catholic, and apostolic Church
- Recognition of canonical Scriptures
- Formation and adoption of the ecumenical creeds
  - Nicene Creed—personhood of Jesus Christ and the reality of the Holy Spirit
  - Apostles' Creed—One God in three persons (Trinity) and God as creator of heaven and earth

Major Beliefs of the Protestant Tradition

- God's grace in Jesus Christ is revealed in Scripture
- Grace alone—God's gift
- Faith alone—not our works
- Scripture alone—no other authority

Five Major Affirmations of the Reformed Faith

1. Election of God's people not only for salvation but also for service
2. Life together marked by disciplined concern for order in the church according to God's Word
3. Faithful stewardship that shuns ostentation and seeks proper use of the gifts of God's creation
4. Recognition of the human tendency to idolatry and tyranny
5. The people of God are called to work for the transformation of society by seeking justice and living in obedience to the Word of God

Six Central Beliefs of the Reformed Tradition

see next page for more detail

1. The Sovereignty of God

2. The Authority of Scripture

3. The Lordship of Jesus Christ

4. Justification by Faith

5. The Priesthood of All Believers

6. The Fellowship of the Church

Sovereignty of God

- There is no part of life that is separate from God
- Every human being at every moment has to do with the living God
- Human life is rooted in the will and intention of God
- The Glory of God and God's purposes in the world are more important than the salvation of one's own soul

The Authority of Scripture

- The Holy Scriptures of the Old and New Testament are the only rule of faith and practice
- The Bible is to be interpreted in light of its witness to God's work of reconciliation in Christ (*BoC* 9.29)

The Lordship of Jesus Christ

- Christ alone is deserving of our allegiance and devotion
- The presence of God in Jesus Christ makes more sense out of life, and gives more meaning to life than any other revelation

Justification by Faith

- We are put right with God by grace through faith alone and not by any thing we are, believe, or do
- Note: the opposite of justification by faith takes two forms: *works righteousness* (where we earn our salvation by being good) and *beliefs righteousness* (where we earn our salvation by believing the right things)—both of which put the responsibility for salvation in humans, not God

The Priesthood of All Believers

- All persons have equal access to God
- No priest (minister) can answer for any human being
- Believers have a right and responsibility to answer for themselves and for their neighbors before God
- There is no qualitative distinction between clergy and lay, sacred and secular, Sunday Christianity and work-week life

The Fellowship of the Church

- You can't be a Christian by yourself; Christianity is corporate as well as personal
- Love of neighbor is the truest test of orthodoxy and doctrine

The Reformed Motto

Ecclesia reformata, semper reformanda

- The Church reformed and always reforming
- Or, the Church reformed and always to be reformed

Comparison to Other Traditions

- Polity
  - Reformed: governance by clergy and elders in representative democracy
  - Episcopalian: hierarchical authority through bishops
  - Congregational: authority vested in individual congregations
- Lord's Supper
  - Reformed: bread and wine are unchanged, but Christ is truly present
  - Catholic: bread and wine are transformed into the body and blood of Jesus

Worksheet 4

THE BIBLE TELLS ME SO

The Understanding of and Use of Holy Scripture

For each of these statements about the Bible, indicate your position using the following scale:

1	2	3	4	5
Strongly Agree	Agree	Not Sure No Opinion	Disagree	Strongly Disagree

(Note: You can change your responses at any time during the discussions)

1. ___ God dictated the words of Scripture to the original authors who recorded them without addition or omission.

2. ___ God inspired the authors of Scripture in such a way as to ensure their writing, shaped by the author's individuality, nevertheless accurately recorded God's word.

3. ___ God used the authors of the Scripture, in their own particular historical and cultural contexts, to communicate God's word for that time and place.

4. ___ God has protected the translations of Scripture through the ages so that what we have in our modern Bibles is the same as God's original words.

5. ___ The Bible is inerrant—completely without error of any kind.

6. ___ The Bible may contain errors and inconsistencies, but only in trivial matters.

7. ___ Apparent errors in the Bible are a result of our limited understanding of God's word.

8. ___ The Bible is a human document. As such it is limited and is subject to errors of both fact and history.

9. ___ The Bible contains errors and inconsistencies, but that does not reduce its capacity to communicate truth.

10. ___ The Bible is a collection of interesting myths, stories, and tales—just like other historical writings—that conveys important truths to every age.

11. ___ Modern knowledge and experience may override biblical understandings and invalidate what the Bible says.

12. ___ The Bible contains everything there is to know about God.

THE BIBLE IN OUR CONFESSIONAL TRADITION

The Confession of 1967
The Bible

9.27 The one sufficient revelation of God is Jesus Christ, the Word of God incarnate, to whom the Holy Spirit bears unique and authoritative witness through the Holy Scriptures, which are received and obeyed as the word of God written. The Scriptures are not a witness among others, but the witness without parallel. The church has received the books of the Old and New Testaments as prophetic and apostolic testimony in which it hears the word of God and by which its faith and obedience are nourished and regulated.

9.28 The New Testament is the recorded testimony of apostles to the coming of the Messiah, Jesus of Nazareth, and the sending of the Holy Spirit to the Church. The Old Testament bears witness to God's faithfulness in his covenant with Israel and points the way to the fulfillment of his purpose in Christ. The Old Testament is indispensable to understanding the New, and is not itself fully understood without the New.

9.29 The Bible is to be interpreted in the light of its witness to God's work of reconciliation in Christ. The Scriptures, given under the guidance of the Holy Spirit, are nevertheless the words of men, conditioned by the language, thought forms, and literary fashions of the places and times at which they were written. They reflect views of life, history, and the cosmos which were then current. The church, therefore, has an obligation to approach the Scriptures with literary and historical understanding. As God has spoken his word in diverse cultural situations, the church is confident that he will continue to speak through the Scriptures in a changing world and in every form of human culture.

9.30 God's word is spoken to his church today where the Scriptures are faithfully preached and attentively read in dependence on the illumination of the Holy Spirit and with readiness to receive their truth and direction.

The Declaration of Faith*
Chapter Six—The Word of God

(3) The Bible is the written Word of God.

Led by the Spirit of God
    the people of Israel and of the early church
    preserved and handed on the story
    of what God had said and done in their midst
    and how they had responded to him.
These traditions were often shaped and reshaped
    by the uses to which the community put them.
They were cherished, written down, and collected
    as the holy literature of the people of God.

Through the inward witness of the same Spirit
    we acknowledge the authority of the Bible.
We accept the Old and New Testaments as the canon,
    or authoritative standard of faith and life,
    to which no further writings need be added.
The Scriptures of the Old and New Testaments
    are necessary, sufficient, and reliable
    as witnesses to Jesus Christ, the living Word.
We must test any word that comes to us
    from church, world, or inner experience
    by the Word of God in Scripture.
We are subject to its judgment
    all our understanding of doctrine and practice,
    including this Declaration of Faith.
We believe the Bible to be the Word of God
    as no other word written by human beings.

Relying on the Holy Spirit,
    who opens our eyes and hearts,
    we affirm our freedom to interpret Scripture
    responsibly.
God has chosen to address his inspired Word to us
    through diverse and varied human writings.
Therefore we use the best available methods
    to understand them in their historical and cultural settings
    and the literary forms in which they are cast.
When we encounter apparent tensions and conflicts
    in what Scripture teaches us to believe and do,
    the final appeal must be to the authority of Christ.
Acknowledging that authority,
    comparing Scripture with Scripture,
    listening with respect to fellow-believers past and present,
    we anticipate that the Holy Spirit
    will enable us to interpret faithfully
    God's Word for our time and place.

*The Declaration of Faith *is not an officially adopted confession but in 1976 it was commended to the Church for study.*

GUIDELINES FOR HOLY SCRIPTURE*

For the Understanding and Use of

1. **Determining What the Text Says**
   a. Use of the Original Languages
   b. Employment of the Best Manuscripts
   c. Priority of the Plain Sense of the Text
      1) Definition of Literary Units
      2) Recognition of the Cultural Conditioning of Language
      3) Understanding of Social and Historical Circumstances
2. **How the Text Is Rightly Used**
   a. Purpose of Holy Scripture
   b. Precedence of Holy Scripture
      1) Priority of Holy Scripture
      2) Use of Knowledge
      3) Use of Experience
   c. Centrality of Jesus Christ
   d. Interpretation of Scripture by Scripture
   e. The Rule of Love
   f. The Rule of Faith
   g. Fallibility of All Interpretation
   h. Relation of Word and Spirit
   i. Use of All Relevant Guidelines

---

*Summaries of
*Presbyterian Understanding and
Use of Holy Scripture*
(A position statement adopted by the
123rd General Assembly [1983] of the
Presbyterian Church in the United States)

and

Biblical Authority and Interpretation
(A resource document received by the 194th
General Assembly [1982] of the United Presbyterian
Church in the United States of America)

For Interpreting

1. Be guided by the basic rules for the interpretation of Scripture that are summarized from the Book of Confessions.
   a. Recognize that Jesus Christ is the center of Scripture.
   b. Let the focus be on the plain text of Scripture, to the grammatical and historical context, rather than to allegory or subjective fantasy.
   c. Depend upon the guidance of the Holy Spirit in interpreting and applying God's message.
   d. Be guided by the doctrinal consensus of the church, which is the rule of faith.
   e. Let all interpretations be in accord with the rule of love, the twofold commandment to love God and to love neighbor.
   f. Remember that interpretation of the Bible requires earnest study in order to establish the best text and to interpret the influence of the historical and cultural context in which the divine message has come.
   g. Seek to interpret a particular passage of the Bible in light of all of the Bible.
2. Recognize that individual perceptions of the truth are always limited and therefore not absolutely authoritative.
3. Realize that points of view are conditioned by points of viewing—try to see the issues from the perspectives of others. Can differences be preserved in ways that lead toward mutual understanding?
4. The preached word must inform the study of the written word—the search for truth includes the life of public prayer and worship.
5. In the immediate situation when controversy arises, locate areas of agreement and disagreement.
   a. Is there agreement as to what biblical passages are relevant to the contemporary issue?
   b. Is there agreement to the meaning of those texts in their original setting?
   c. Is there agreement as to how these texts should be applied to the present situation?
   d. Is there agreement as to what the Christian tradition in general and the Reformed tradition in particular have taught concerning this issue?
6. In potentially long-term controversies, covenant together to study the Bible in regard to the issue—ensuring openness to differing opinions.
7. Together try to determine the range of options that are open to the church for speech and action in regard to the contemporary situation.
8. Rely on the democratic process of the denomination in assemblies. Use the established channels of communication and the process of voting to express conviction, either as part of the majority or the minority. Be willing to accept decisions and welcome the continuing advocacy of minority view.

Worksheet 5

WORSHIP AND SACRAMENTS QUIZ (TRUE OR FALSE)

_____ 1. "There can be no worship without mission and outreach."*

_____ 2. "Being in a particular structure, familiar or not, does not guarantee that people will be treated with Christian love or respect."**

_____ 3. "As church officers we are especially responsible to the church in our prayer life."***

_____ 4. Presbyterians celebrate four sacraments: the Lord's Supper, Baptism, Weddings, and Funerals.

_____ 5. A sacrament is a holy ordinance instituted by Christ.

_____ 6. All children are eligible for baptism.

_____ 7. A child being baptized in a Presbyterian church must have parents who are members of a Presbyterian church.

_____ 8. No one can be excluded from the Lord's Table.

_____ 9. Children are not allowed to partake of the Lord's Supper until they are confirmed.

_____ 10. Artistic expressions (architecture, furnishings, music, drama, etc.) should evoke, edify, and enhance the worshiper's need for comfort and reassurance of grace.

_____ 11. Those responsible for worship are to be guided by the Reformed tradition, the tradition of the local congregation, and openness to diversity and inclusive language.

_____ 12. In a particular church, the clergy are to provide for worship and shall encourage the people to participate fully and regularly in it.

_____ 13. The session has authority to choose Scriptures and lessons to be read, to oversee the prayers offered on behalf of the people, and to choose the music to be sung.

_____ 14. The sequence or proportion of the elements of worship are the responsibility of the session with the concurrence of the pastor.

_____ 15. The sermon is the heart of worship.

_____ 16. In worship, music is not to be for entertainment or artistic display.

_____ 17. The minister of the Word and Sacrament has responsibility for the selection of the version of text from which the Scripture lessons are read in public worship.

_____ 18. The congregation may read Scripture responsively, antiphonally, or in unison as a part of the service.

_____ 19. Only a minister can invite another minister to preach in his or her pulpit.

_____ 20. It is possible to be rebaptized if someone has a conversion experience.

_____ 21. Baptism is authorized by the clergy and can be celebrated in private or public worship.

_____ 22. The session assumes responsibility for nurturing the baptized person in the Christian life.

_____ 23. It is appropriate to celebrate the Lord's Supper as often as each Lord's day.

* Johnson, _Selected to Serve,_ 53.
** Johnson, 59.
*** Johnson, 61.

WORSHIP AND SACRAMENTS QUIZ KEY

True   1. "There can be no worship without mission and outreach."*

True   2. "Being in a particular structure, familiar or not, does not guarantee that people will be treated with Christian love or respect."**

True   3. "As church officers we are especially responsible to the church in our prayer life."***

False   4. Presbyterians celebrate four sacraments: the Lord's Supper, Baptism, Weddings, and Funerals.

     Presbyterians celebrate only two sacraments: the Lord's Supper and Baptism.

True   5. A sacrament is a holy ordinance instituted by Christ.

False   6. All children are eligible for baptism.

     Children of believers are to be baptized without undue delay, but without undue haste. (BoO W-2.3008)

False   7. A child being baptized in a Presbyterian church must have parents who are members of a Presbyterian church.

     When a child is being presented for Baptism, ordinarily the parent(s) or one(s) rightly exercising parental responsibility shall be an active member of the congregation. The session may also consider a request for the Baptism of the child from a Christian parent who is an active member of another congregation. (BoO W-2.3014)

False   8. No one can be excluded from the Lord's Table.

     All the baptized faithful are to be welcomed to the Table, and none should be excluded because of race, sex, age, economic status, social class, handicapping condition, difference of culture or language, or any barrier created by human injustice. (BoO W-2.4006)

False   9. Children are not allowed to partake of the Lord's Supper until they are confirmed.

     Baptized children who are being nurtured and instructed by the significance of the invitation to the Table and the meaning of their response are invited to receive the Lord's Supper, recognizing that their understanding of participation will vary according to their maturity. (BoO W-4.2002)

False 10. Artistic expressions (architecture, furnishings, music, drama, etc.) should evoke, edify, and enhance the worshiper's need for comfort and reassurance of grace.

     Artistic expressions should evoke, edify, enhance, and expand the worshiper's consciousness of the reality and grace of God. (BoO W-1.3034.2)

False 11. Those responsible for worship are to be guided by the Reformed tradition, the tradition of the local congregation, and openness to diversity and inclusive language.

     Those responsible for worship are to be guided by the Holy Spirit speaking in Scripture, the historic experience of the Church universal, the Reformed tradition, the Book of Confessions, *the needs and particular circumstances of the worshiping community, as well as the provisions of the form of government and this directory. (BoO W-1.4001)*

   * Johnson, *Selected to Serve,* 53.
  ** Johnson, 59.
 *** Johnson, 61.

False 12. In a particular church, the clergy are to provide for worship and shall encourage the people to participate fully and regularly in it.

In a particular church, the session is to provide for worship and shall encourage the people to participate fully and regularly in it. (BoO W-1.4004)

False 13. The session has authority to choose Scriptures and lessons to be read, to oversee the prayers offered on behalf of the people, and to choose the music to be sung.

The minister has authority to choose Scriptures and lessons to be read, to oversee the prayers offered on behalf of the people, and to choose the music to be sung. (BoO W-1.4005a)

False 14. The sequence or proportion of the elements of worship are the responsibility of the session with the concurrence of the pastor.

The sequence or proportion of the elements of worship are the responsibility of the pastor with the concurrence of the session. (BoO W-1.4006)

False 15. The sermon is the heart of worship.

Prayer is the heart of worship. (BoO W-2.1001)

True 16. In worship, music is not to be for entertainment or artistic display. (*BoO* W-2.1004)

True 17. The minister of the Word and Sacrament has responsibility for the selection of the version of text from which the Scripture lessons are read in public worship. (*BoO* W-2.2005)

True 18. The congregation may read Scripture responsively, antiphonally, or in unison as a part of the service. (*BoO* W-2.2006)

False 19. Only a minister can invite another minister to preach in his or her pulpit.

A minister of the Word and Sacrament or other person authorized by the presbytery may be invited by the pastor with the concurrence of the session, or when there is no pastor, by the session. (BoO W-2.2007)

False 20. It is possible to be rebaptized if someone has a conversion experience.

Baptism is received only once. (BoO W-2.3009)

False 21. Baptism is authorized by the clergy and can be celebrated in private or public worship.

Baptism is celebrated in a service of public worship. (BoO W-2.3011)

False 22. The session assumes responsibility for nurturing the baptized person in the Christian life.

The congregation assumes responsibility for nurturing the baptized person in the Christian life. (BoO W-2.3013)

True 23. It is appropriate to celebrate the Lord's Supper as often as each Lord's day. (*BoO* W-2.4009)

Worksheet 6

To Be or Not to Be—Reformed!

Adapted from an activity in *The Roots of Who We Are*, by Rodger Nishioka, Bridge Resources, Louisville, Ky., 1997

Step 1: In the column marked "I" evaluate each of the following statements or viewpoints using the following scale:

3 = **Definitely** a Presbyterian/Reformed point of view

2 = **Don't know**/can't tell/could be . . .

1 = **Definitely NOT** a Presbyterian/Reformed point of view

I	G	R	Statement or Viewpoint
			1. Human beings are certainly sinful, but God has given humans the freedom to choose between good and evil.
			2. Infants should be baptized as soon as possible so that, if they were to die, they would still be saved and go to heaven.
			3. When you stop your busyness and really focus on listening, then God will speak to you.
			4. Christians should stay out of politics and social issues and focus on developing their own personal relationship to Jesus Christ.
			5. God spoke to humans through the divine words written down as Scripture and has preserved them to reveal God's truth for every age.
			6. The first priority of Christians is to share the good news with others and lead them to Christ.
			7. If we, after helping ourselves as much as we can, reach out to God, God is ready and waiting to help and will reach out to us.
			8. I don't have to go to church to be spiritual, and being a spiritual person is more important that being religious.
			9. Why should I bother going to church if the church isn't meeting my spiritual needs?
			10. The problem with many Christians today is they spend too much energy on trying to make sense of their faith instead of just experiencing God and living their faith.
			11. God looks at the motivations in our hearts. If we try our best and do more good than bad in this life, God will honor our intentions and reward us in heaven.
			12. If people would only read the Bible, they would find answers to all their questions about modern life.

You will be given instructions for additional steps and the use of the other columns in class.

SOME ESSENTIAL TENETS OF THE REFORMED FAITH
From **Book of Order** *G-2.0300–G-2.0500*

Tradition	Tenet/Belief/Doctrine
CATHOLIC (universal)	1. **Trinity**— the mystery of the triune God
	2. **Incarnation**— of the eternal Word of God in Jesus Christ
PROTESTANT	3. **Justification by grace through faith**— grace alone, faith alone
	4. **Scripture** reveals God's grace in Jesus Christ— Scripture alone
REFORMED	5. **Sovereignty of God**— the majesty, holiness, and providence of God who creates, sustains, rules, and redeems the world in the freedom of sovereign righteousness and love
	6. **Election for service and salvation**— love of neighbor as well as love of God
	7. **Covenant life**— marked by disciplined concern for order in the church according to the Word of God
	8. **Stewardship**— that shuns ostentation and seeks proper use of the gifts of God's creation
	9. **Human tendency toward idolatry and tyranny**— which calls the people of God to work for the transformation of society by seeking justice and living in obedience to the Word of God

CONSTITUTIONAL QUESTIONS TO OFFICERS

The minister shall ask those preparing to be ordained or installed to stand before the congregation and to answer the following questions (G-14.0207):

QUESTION		CONTENT AREA
G-14.0207a.	1) Do you trust in Jesus Christ your Savior, acknowledge him Lord of all and Head of the Church, and through him believe in one God, Father, Son, and Holy Spirit?	**Personal Faith**
G-14.0207b.	2) Do you accept the Scriptures of the Old and New Testaments to be, by the Holy Spirit, the unique and authoritative witness to Jesus Christ in the Church universal, and God's Word to you?	**Doctrine** The Authority of Scripture
G-14.0207c.	3) Do you sincerely receive and adopt the essential tenets of the Reformed faith as expressed in the confessions of our church as authentic and reliable expositions of what Scripture leads us to believe and do, and will you be instructed and led by those confessions as you lead the people of God?	**Doctrine** Theology, the Confessions, and Authority in the Church
G-14.0207d.	4) Will you fulfill your office in obedience to Jesus Christ, under the authority of Scripture, and be continually guided by our confessions?	
G-14.0207e.	5) Will you be governed by our church's polity, and will you abide by its discipline? Will you be a friend among your colleagues in ministry, working with them, subject to the ordering of God's Word and Spirit?	**Governance and Discipline**
G-14.0207f.	6) Will you in your own life seek to follow the Lord Jesus Christ, love your neighbors, and work for the reconciliation of the world?	**Individual Commitment**
G-14.0207g.	7) Do you promise to further the peace, unity, and purity of the church?	
G-14.0207h.	8) Will you seek to serve the people with energy, intelligence, imagination, and love?	
G-14.0207i.	9) (*For elder*) Will you be a faithful elder, watching over the people, providing for their worship, nurture, and service? Will you share in government and discipline, serving in governing bodies of the church, and in your ministry will you try to show the love and justice of Jesus Christ?	**Duties of the Office**
G-14.0207j.	9) (*For deacon*) Will you be a faithful deacon, teaching charity, urging concern, and directing the people's help to the friendless and those in need? In your ministry will you try to show the love and justice of Jesus Christ?	

Worksheet 7

CONSTITUTIONAL QUESTIONS TO OFFICERS WORKSHEET

Book of Order G-14.0207

For each question record a number that represents where you are on this scale:

Great Reservation	1 . . . . 2 . . . . 3 . . . . 4 . . . . 5 . . . . 6 7	Great Enthusiasm
	- - -　　　　- -　　　　-　　　　-/+　　　　+　　　　++　　　　+++	

- 1 = I am troubled by this question and/or could not answer "yes" without additional explanation
- 2, 3 = Decreasing difficulty
- 4 = I have no difficulties nor enthusiasm in my answer to this question
- 5, 6 = Increasing enthusiasm
- 7 = I can enthusiastically and without reservation say "yes" to this question

#	Constitutional Question	References[1]
a.	Do you trust in Jesus Christ your Savior, acknowledge him Lord of all and Head of the Church, and through him believe in one God, Father, Son, and Holy Spirit?	1 Cor. 12:12–26; Col. 1:15–20; Eph. 4:11–16 *BoC*: 6.043–6.050; 9.08–9.14; 10.2 *BoO*: G-1.0100; G-1.0307
b.	Do you accept the Scriptures of the Old and New Testaments to be, by the Holy Spirit, the unique and authoritative witness to Jesus Christ in the Church universal, and God's Word to you?	2 Tim. 3:16–17; Acts 17:11, 18:28 *BoC*: 5.001–009; 6.001–6.010; 9.27–9.30 *BoO*: G-1.0307; W-2.2000
c.	Do you sincerely receive and adopt the essential tenets of the Reformed faith as expressed in the confessions of our church as authentic and reliable expositions of what Scripture leads us to believe and do, and will you be instructed and led by those confessions as you lead the people of God?	*BoO*: G-2
d.	Will you fulfill your office in obedience to Jesus Christ, under the authority of Scripture, and be continually guided by our confessions?	
e.	Will you be governed by our church's polity, and will you abide by its discipline? Will you be a friend among your colleagues in ministry, working with them, subject to the ordering of God's Word and Spirit?	*BoC*: 9.34–9.40; 6.196–6.172 *BoO*: G-1; 3; 4.0300; 6.0100; 9
f.	Will you in your own life seek to follow the Lord Jesus Christ, love your neighbors, and work for the reconciliation of the world?	*BoO*: G-3; 4.0400; 5.0100; 6.0200, 6.0300, 6.0400; W-6, 7
g.	Do you promise to further the peace, unity, and purity of the church?	*BoC*: 6.169–6.172; 9.34–9.40; 5.132–135, 140, 141; 10.4 *BoO*: G-1.0200; 3.0400; 4.0200, .0302, .0303; 4.0400; W-7
h.	Will you seek to serve the people with energy, intelligence, imagination, and love?	*BoO*: G-3; 4.0400; 5.0100; 6.0200, 6.0300, 6.0400; W-6, 7
i.	**(For elder)** Will you be a faithful elder, watching over the people, providing for their worship, nurture, and service? Will you share in government and discipline, serving in governing bodies of the church, and in your ministry will you try to show the love and justice of Jesus Christ?	1 Tim. 3:1–13; Titus 1:5–9 *BoO*: G-4.0300–4.0400; 6.0100
j.	**(For deacon)** Will you be a faithful deacon, teaching charity, urging concern, and directing the people's help to the friendless and those in need? In your ministry will you try to show the love and justice of Jesus Christ?	

From Howard L. Rice and Calvin Chinn, *The Ordination Questions: A Study for Church Officers* (Louisville, Ky.: Geneva Press, 1996).

Worksheet 8

BOOK OF CONFESSIONS WORKSHEET

Confession	Date(s)	Location	Historical Context/Issues/Themes
Nicene Creed			
Apostles' Creed			
Scots Confession			
Heidelberg Catechism			
Second Helvetic Confession			
Westminster Confession			
Shorter Catechism			
Larger Catechism			
Theological Declaration of Barmen			
Confession of 1967			
Brief Statement of Faith			

BOOK OF CONFESSIONS WORKSHEET KEY

Confession	Date(s)	Location	Historical Context/Issues/Themes
Nicene Creed	325 381	Nicaea Constantinople	Constantine, Roman Emperor, converted to Christianity, sought to address disputes Nature of Christ—was the divinity of Christ *created* by God or the *same as* God?
Apostles' Creed	180 2nd/3rd c. 4th/5th c. 5th c. 8th c.	Rome Rome N. Africa Gaul	Marcionite heresy: Jesus was not OT Messiah Forgiveness of sins Holy, catholic church He descended into hell (finalized as we know it)
Scots Confession	1560	Scotland	Scottish Parliament declares Scotland a Protestant nation; commissions new confession of faith; John Knox; emphasizes God's providence and calls for trust and commitment in turbulent times
Heidelberg Catechism	1562–63	Germany	Tension between Reformed and Lutheran movements: nature of Christ's presence in Lord's Supper; creed states what both can affirm; based on Romans 7:24–25
Second Helvetic Confession	1561	Switzerland	Swiss-German Reformed Church Bullinger wrote it as part of his Last Will and Testament; used by Frederick (Governor) as defense; adopted by churches of Switzerland
Westminster Confession	1647 1647 1729 1903	England Scotland America (addendum)	English government called for settling issues of church governance and liturgy; Westminster Assembly convened; political and religious conflicts; civil war; adopted later by other countries
Shorter Catechism	1649	England	Westminster Assembly (above)
Larger Catechism	1649	England	Westminster Assembly (above)
Theological Declaration of Barmen	1934	Germany	Rise of Nazi Germany, WWII; equating nationalism, militarism, and patriotism (under Hitler) with Christianity; there is only one Lord, Jesus Christ, who is Lord over every area of life
Confession of 1967	1967	USA UPC(USA)	Turbulent 1960s; concurrent with Vatican II; prompted by request to revise the Westminster Confession; themes of reconciliation and the Church's role in the world; addressed need to interpret Scripture; *Book of Confessions* adopted
Brief Statement of Faith	1983	USA	Reunion of northern and southern branches of Presbyterianism in USA to form PC(USA); articulates common identity in midst of diversity and disagreement; gender inclusiveness, care for God's creation; "In life and in death, we belong to God"

Appendix E

SMALL-GROUP WORKSHEETS

My Models of Faith

In column I, write the names of persons who have been models of faith for you. List the most significant according to the prescribed age category. In column II, briefly explain why you consider them a model of faith. In column III, list the characteristics you have "adopted" from your model. What did you take from them? Also list what you did not take in the process of establishing your own faith.

	Column I	Column II	Column III	
	Models of Faith *Name Individuals*	Explain Why They Are Models	What I "Adopted" from Them	What I Did Not "Adopt" from Them
C H I L D H O O D 0–14				
Y O U T H 14–20				
E A R L Y A D U L T 20–35				

	Column I	Column II	Column III	
	Models of Faith *Name Individuals*	Explain Why They Are Models	What I "Adopted" from Them	What I Did Not "Adopt" from Them
M I D D L E A D U L T 35–55				
L A T E R A D U L T 55+				

To Be a Christian

Instructions:

Write out all of your responses in order to help you think through the questions. As a group, go around the room and allow each person to choose one of the questions he/she would like to share with the group. As time allows, keep going around the room, selecting more questions from each member of the group.

1. Why do you call yourself a Christian?

2. How did you come to be a Christian?

3. Who or what has been the single most important influence in your Christian life?

4. What has been the most important truth about God in shaping your Christian life?

_____

_____

_____

_____

_____

_____

5. What urges to grow do you feel?

_____

_____

_____

_____

_____

_____

6. What anxieties, questions, or resistances do you feel in relationship to growth in your life with God?

_____

_____

_____

_____

_____

_____

From Robert H. Ramey Jr. and Ben Campbell Johnson, *Living the Christian Life: A Guide to Reformed Spirituality* (Louisville, Ky.: Westminster/John Knox Press, 1992), 163.

My Faith Inventory

1. My first recollection of being in church is . . .

_____

_____

_____

_____

2. I was baptized in the _____

Church by _____

when I was _____ years old.

3. The closest I have ever felt to God in my life was . . .

_____

_____

_____

_____

4. The time I have felt the greatest doubt or distance from God was . . .

_____

_____

_____

_____

5. Just before I die I want to be able to say . . .

_____

_____

_____

_____

_____

My Reflections and Goals for Faith Development

This worksheet guides you in setting some personal goals in further developing your faith, which will in turn enhance the ministry of this church.

Please prayerfully consider your responses.

1. This course has made me aware of . . .

_____

_____

_____

_____

_____

2. As an elder/deacon, I feel a need to . . .

_____

_____

_____

_____

_____

3. I would love to see our church . . .

_____

_____

_____

_____

_____

4. I need to deepen my commitment by . . .

_____

_____

_____

_____

_____

5. What I appreciate about time in small group was . . .

_____

_____

_____

_____

_____

6. I need to grow in . . .

_____

_____

_____

_____

_____

7. A goal I am setting for myself in my walk with Christ is . . .

_____

_____

_____

_____

_____

8. Would you like to share anything else with the group in this final meeting?

_____

_____

_____

_____

_____

9. Please close the meeting with prayer together.

Appendix F

MISCELLANEOUS CORRESPONDENCE AND FORMS

Sample Letter to the Table Moderators
from the Officer Education Committee

TO: Table Moderators
FROM: Officer Education Committee
DATE: April 21, 2003

THANK You—for offering to serve as a table moderator for the exam dinner on April 28, 2003, beginning at 5:30 p.m. in Providence Hall.

Schedule for the evening—

> 5:30 p.m. Dinner (cost: $6.00, payable at the door)
>
> 6:25 p.m. Session meeting convened
>
> 6:30 p.m. Exam
>
> 7:15 p.m. Break
>
> 7:30 p.m. Reconvene session meeting for business and Communion

Exam questions and answers—Attached you will find the questions the incoming officers have been asked to prepare for along with the appropriate answers.

Moderating the exam—here are some suggestions:

- Set a nonthreatening climate, even though this is a serious task.

- You will begin the exam time by hearing individual faith statements. *Please collect the written statements.* Be affirming of each statement without getting into a discussion about them. Thank each person for sharing and move on to the next person.

- Next, move into the questions. Be aware that you will not have time to cover all the questions. Come prepared with the questions marked that you most wish to cover. The incoming officers are allowed to have their notes with them for reference if necessary. Discourage any verbatim reading from their notes.

- You control the amount of time to be spent on each question. It seems better to pose the questions to an individual rather than to the group at-large. Otherwise, the confident ones will always jump in. Remember that you will have some experienced officers as well as first-time officers.

What to do with a wrong answer?

- Clarify the question, ask it in a different way, or have them refer to their notes.

- Invite another person to say how she or he would answer the question.

- Always affirm the person even if you can't affirm the answer they gave.

Involving other elders in the exam—

- Ask an elder to monitor the clock and to help keep things moving so that every officer-elect has an opportunity to participate fully in the entire examination.

- If other elders start answering the questions themselves, gently remind them that it's important to hear the responses of the officers-elect; they can be invited to add their thoughts at the end of the exam.

- Thank them for their contribution and assume leadership for moving along.

Immediately following the exam—You will report to the church officer education committee, which will bring the appropriate motion to the session: 1) whether all persons examined should be approved or 2) whether there are any questions as to the preparation or readiness of any officer-elect to serve.

Writing Your Faith Statement

Each officer-elect will write a statement of her or his personal faith. This faith statement will be shared verbally with other officers-elect and examining elders at the session examination. A faith statement is not a telling of their faith journey ("I grew up in a Christian home") but rather more like a "confession" articulating the content of what you believe as a person of faith. It is often in the form of "I believe . . . ," although many creative forms are possible. Your pastor or leader may have for your review samples of statements of faith from previous officer development classes.

A faith statement will often include, *but not be limited to*, specific statements of belief in the following areas:

- God
- Jesus Christ
- The Holy Spirit
- The Bible
- The Church
- The role of Christians in this world
- One's own personal sense of call, purpose, or mission in the world

Officer Training—Evaluation

Name: _____

Office (Deacon or Elder) _____

Have you been previously ordained to this office? _____ yes _____ no

1. Which part of the training was most beneficial for you? (Check one)

    _____ Worship/Communion   _____ Theology

    _____ Assigned Readings   _____ Polity

    _____ Small Groups   _____ Other

    Comments:

    _____

    _____

    _____

2. What would you suggest needs improving for future classes?

    _____

    _____

    _____

3. Did you complete all the reading assignments? Yes _____ No _____

4. Do you think more sessions are needed for training? Or do you think four sessions are adequate? Explain:

    _____

    _____

    _____

5. How would you rank the course in terms of overall organization (preparation, general flow, mechanics, etc.)? (Circle one.)

    $$1 \ldots 2 \ldots 3 \ldots 4 \ldots 5$$
    Low   High

    Comments:

    _____

    _____

6. My most significant learning/experience in this course was . . .

_____

_____

_____

7. How would you rank the facilitators' roles in this training course?

1 . . . . 2 . . . . 3 . . . . 4 5
Low   High

8. Do you feel more prepared to take office after the training course?

Yes _____ No _____

Explain:

_____

_____

_____

9. Is there any area in which you sense you need more training **before or after** taking office?

Explain:

_____

_____

_____

10. Other suggestions, comments?

_____

_____

_____

Thank you for completing this form and for accepting God's call to serve.

Appendix G

RESOURCES FOR CHURCH OFFICER DEVELOPMENT

Books

A list of titles to aid in church officer development is provided at the end of this book, after the endnotes.

Videos

Who Are We Presbyterians?
$17.95—available from Presbyterian Marketplace
Included in this seventeen-minute video are vivid portrayals of what it means to be Presbyterian. Excellent tool for church school, church officer training, new members' classes, and many other occasions. It includes a study guide written by former Moderator Freda Gardner.

Across the Centuries: The Church Constitution Today
$24.97—Interlink Video Products
A ten-minute introduction to the Constitution of the PC(USA).

In Spirit and In Truth: The Directory for Worship
$24.95—Interlink Video Products
A twenty-minute introduction to the Directory of Worship.

To All Generations
$24.95—Interlink Video Products
A forty-minute overview of *The Book of Confessions*.

Note: Videos from Interlink Video Products may be ordered by calling 1-800-662-1151.

Online

www.pcusa.org
The PC(USA) denominational website. News and information about Presbyterian missions, doctrinal beliefs and practices, stands on social issues, and links to periodicals and the Presbyterian Marketplace.

www.pres-outlook.com
An independent weekly magazine providing news and analysis of life in the Presbyterian Church and its work and witness in the world.

Biblical References

Chapter 1

Exodus 18:17–18, 22b–23
Exodus 18:18
Exodus 18:23
Numbers 11:12, 14–15
Numbers 11:16–17
Matthew 28:19–20
Mark 6:30–44
Mark 6:37
Mark 6:38
Mark 6:41

Chapter 2

Numbers 11:16
Ephesians 4:1–16

Chapter 4

Genesis 12:1–9	The call of Abram/Sarai
Genesis 22:1–18	The test of Abraham
Exodus 3:1–14	The call of Moses
Exodus 14:10–31	The Red Sea
Exodus 16	The manna
Exodus 18	Jethro's advice
Exodus 32	The golden calf
Exodus 33:7–23	The tent of meeting
Numbers 11:4–17	The seventy elders

Deuteronomy 8:10–20	Don't forget
Judges 6	Gideon—being reduced
1 Samuel 16	The call of David
2 Chronicles 7:11–16	"If My People . . ."
Job 38–42 (selected)	Knowing your place
Psalm 51	The sins of leadership
Ecclesiastes 3:1–8	Timing
Jeremiah 32:1–15	Jeremiah's field
Micah 6:8	What does the Lord require?
Malachi 3:6–12	The tithe
Matthew 4:1–11	The temptation of Jesus
Matthew 8:18–22	The cost of discipleship
Matthew 10:1–42	Sending of the Twelve
Matthew 13:24–30	Parable of the weeds
Matthew 19:13–15	Jesus and children
Matthew 19:16–30	Young rich ruler
Mark 4:1–20	The parable of the sower
Mark 6:30–44	Feeding of five thousand
Luke 5:17–26	Healing of a paralytic
Luke 10:38–42	Mary and Martha
Luke 21:1–4	The widow's example
Luke 24:1–12	The resurrection
John 3:1–21	Nicodemus
John 15:1–17	The vine and the branches
Acts 2	Pentecost
Acts 7:54–60	The stoning of Stephen
Acts 9:1–9	Saul's conversion
Ephesians 4:1–16	The offices of leadership
1 Timothy 3:1–13	Qualifications for the office
James 5:13–16	Prayer

Appendix A

Numbers 11:10–17
Isaiah 40:28–29
Mark 6:30–44
Acts 1:8, 2:1–4, 43–47

Notes

Introduction

1. Stephen Covey, *The Seven Habits of Highly Effective People* (New York: Simon & Schuster Inc., 1989), 98.

2. William H. Willimon, *Pastor* (Nashville: Abingdon Press, 2002), 22.

3. Presbyterian Church (U.S.A.), *Book of Order, 2001–2002* (Louisville, Ky.: Published by The Office of the General Assembly), G-14.0205.

4. Background Survey for the 2000–2002 Presbyterian Panel, available at http://www.pcusa.org/research/panel/bkg2000.htm.

5. Background Survey for the 2003–2005 Presbyterian Panel, available at http://www.pcusa.org/research/panel/.

Chapter 2

1. Anthony B. Robinson, *Transforming Congregational Culture* (Grand Rapids: William B. Eerdmans Publishing Co., 2003).

2. Presbyterian Church (U.S.A.), *Called to Serve: A Workbook for Training Nominating Committees and Church Officers*, Eugene Witherspoon and Marvin Simmers, eds. (Louisville, Ky.: Congregational Ministries Publishing, 1997).

3. Ibid., 2.9–2.11.

4. Edward K. Fretz, *Nominating Church Officers*, rev. Marvin L. Simmers (Louisville, Ky.: Presbyterian Publishing House, 1993).

Chapter 5

1. Adapted from *The Kerygma Program Guide,* published by The Kerygma Program, 300 Mount Lebanon Boulevard, Suite 205, Pittsburgh, Penn. 15234.

Chapter 6

1. The Presbyterian Marketplace is one-stop center for all things Presbyterian. Phone: 800-524-2612; Internet: http://www.pcusa.org/marketplace/index.jsp

2. References to specific websites change over time. At the time of this writing, the paper could be found at http://www.pcusa.org/pcusa/cmd/cfl/christdoc.htm

3. Earl S. Johnson, *Witness without Parallel—Eight Biblical Texts That Make Us Presbyterian* (Louisville, Ky.: Geneva Press, 2003).

4. Adopted by the 210th General Assembly (1998) of the PC(USA) and commended to the church for study and reflection. This document is not an officially approved confession, but it does speak a confessional word to today's church. Copies may be ordered from the Presbyterian Marketplace noted above or may be downloaded from the Internet at http://www.pcusa.org/catech/studycat.htm.

5. Rodger Nishioka, *The Roots of Who We Are* (Louisville, Ky.: Bridge Resources, 1997).

6. Howard L. Rice and Calvin Chinn, *The Ordination Questions . . . a Study for Church Officers* (Louisville, Ky.: Geneva Press, 1996).

Chapter 7

1. John Calvin, *Golden Booklet of the True Christian Life* (Grand Rapids: Baker, 1952), 17.

2. Neil F. McBride, *How to Lead Small Groups* (Colorado Springs, Colo.: Navpress, 1990), 57–58.

Chapter 9

1. Anthony B. Robinson, *Transforming Congregational Culture* (Grand Rapids: William B. Eerdmans Publishing Co., 2003).

Chapter 10

1. Earl S. Johnson, *Witness without Parallel: Eight Biblical Texts That Make Us Presbyterian* (Louisville, Ky.: Geneva Press, 2003).

2. Guy D. Griffith, *Devotion and Discipline: Training for Presbyterian Leaders* (Louisville, Ky.: Geneva Press, 1999).

Books to Aid in
Church Officer Development

Book of Confessions: The Constitution of the Presbyterian Church (U.S.A.), Part 1. Louisville, Ky.: The Office of the General Assembly, 1999.

Book of Order 2003/2004. The Constitution of the Presbyterian Church (U.S.A.), Part 2. Louisville, Ky.: The Office of the General Assembly, 2003.

Angell, James W. *How to Spell Presbyterian.* Rev. ed. Louisville, Ky.: Geneva Press, 2002.

Beattie, Frank A. *Companion to the Constitution of the Presbyterian Church (U.S.A.): Polity for the Local Church.* Louisville, Ky.: Geneva Press, 1999.

Bruce, Barbara. *Our Spiritual Brain.* Nashville: Abingdon Press, 2002.

Bush, Michael D., and Zeta T. Lamberson. *Foundations of Faith: Education for New Church Members (Student Guide).* Louisville, Ky.: Geneva Press, 1999.

———. *Foundations of Faith: Education for New Church Members (Teacher's Guide).* Louisville, Ky.: Geneva Press, 1999.

Chapman, William E. *History and Theology in the Book of Order: Blood on Every Page.* Louisville, Ky.: Witherspoon Press, 1999.

Eberts, Harry W., Jr. *We Believe: A Study of the Book of Confessions for Church Officers.* Rev. ed. Louisville, Ky.: Westminster John Knox Press, 1994.

Foote, Ted V., Jr., and P. Alex Thornburg. *Being Disciples of Jesus in a Dot.Com World: A Theological Survival Guide for Youth, Adults, and Other Confused Christians.* Louisville, Ky.: Westminster John Knox Press, 2003.

———. *Being Presbyterian in the Bible Belt: A Theological Survival Guide for Youth, Parents, and Other Confused Christians.* Louisville, Ky.: Geneva Press, 2000.

Gray, Joan S., and Joyce C. Tucker. *Presbyterian Polity for Church Officers: Third Edition.* Louisville, Ky.: Geneva Press, 1999.

Griffith, Guy D. *Devotion and Discipline: Training for Presbyterian Leaders.* Louisville, Ky.: Geneva Press, 1999.

Guthrie, Shirley C., Jr. *Always Being Reformed: Faith for a Fragmented World.* Louisville, Ky.: Westminster John Knox Press, 1996.

———. *Christian Doctrine.* Louisville, Ky.: Westminster John Knox Press, 1994.

Hassall, Harry S. *Presbyterians: People of the Middle Way (Student Text).* Franklin, Tenn.: Providence House Publishers, 1996.

———. *Presbyterians: People of the Middle Way (Teacher's Guide).* Franklin, Tenn.: Providence House Publishers, 1996.

Johnson, Earl S., Jr. *The Presbyterian Deacon: An Essential Guide.* Louisville, Ky.: Geneva Press, 2002.

———. *Selected to Serve: A Guide for Church Officers.* Louisville, Ky.: Geneva Press, 2000.

———. *Witness without Parallel: Eight Biblical Texts That Make Us Presbyterian.* Louisville, Ky.: Geneva Press, 2003.

Leith, John H. *Basic Christian Doctrine.* Louisville, Ky.: Westminster/John Knox Press, 1993.

McKim, Donald K. *Introducing the Reformed Faith: Biblical Revelation, Christian Tradition, Contemporary Significance.* Louisville, Ky.: Westminster John Knox Press, 2001.

Melander, Rochelle, and Harold Eppley. *Growing Together: Spiritual Exercises for Church Committees.* Minneapolis: Augsburg Fortress Press, 1998.

Mulder, John M. *Sealed in Christ: The Symbolism of the Seal of the Presbyterian Church (U.S.A.).* Louisville, Ky.: Geneva Press, 1991.

Nishioka, Rodger. *The Roots of Who We Are.* Louisville, Ky.: Bridge Resources, 1997.

Olsen, Charles M. *Transforming Church Board into Communities of Spiritual Leaders.* Alban Institute Publication, 1995.

Palmer, Parker J. *Leading from Within.* Washington, D.C.: The Potter's House Book Service, 1990.

Placher, William C., and David Willis-Watkins. *Belonging to God: A Commentary on A Brief Statement of Faith.* Louisville, Ky.: Westminster/John Knox Press, 1992.

Plunkett, Stephen W. *This We Believe: Eight Truths Presbyterians Affirm.* Louisville, Ky.: Geneva Press, 2002.

Rice, Howard L., and Calvin Chinn. *The Ordination Questions: A Study for Church Officers.* Louisville, Ky.: Geneva Press, 1996.

Rogers, Jack. *Presbyterian Creeds: A Guide to the Book of Confessions.* Louisville, Ky.: Westminster/John Knox Press, 1991.

Witherspoon, Eugene, and Marvin Simmers, eds. *Called to Serve: A Workbook for Training Nominating Committees and Church Officers.* Louisville, Ky.: Curriculum Publishing, Presbyterian Church (U.S.A.), 1997.

Wright, Paul S. *The Presbyterian Elder.* Rev. ed. Louisville, Ky.: Geneva Press, 1992.

Made in the USA
Lexington, KY
01 December 2009